CHICAGO PUBLIC LIBRARY
HAROLD WASHINGTON LIBRARY CENTER

R0031143035

D1000727

CORE COLLECTION

DISCARD

REF
BF
723
.P25
B53

Biller, Henry B.

Father, child,
and sex role

DATE DUE

CORE COLLECTION			
DO NOT SPECIAL LOAN			

FORM 125 M

Cop. 1   SOCIAL SCIENCES AND HISTORY DIVISION

The Chicago Public Library

Received___MAR 2 9 1977___

DISCARD

Father, Child,
and Sex Role

Lexington Books
in Psychology
under the general editorship of
Paul H. Mussen
and
Mark R. Rosenzweig
University of California
Berkeley

Father, Child, and Sex Role

Paternal Determinants of Personality Development

1971

Henry B. Biller
University of Rhode Island

Heath Lexington Books
D.C. Heath and Company
Lexington, Massachusetts

REF
BF
723
.P25
B53

Cop. 1

Soc

Copyright © *1971 by D.C. Heath and Company*

All rights reserved. No part of this publication may be reproduced or transmitted in any form or by any means, electronic or mechanical, including photocopy, recording, or any information storage or retrieval system, without permission in writing from the publisher.

Third printing, October 1973.

Published simultaneously in Canada.

Printed in the United States of America.

Library of Congress Catalog Card Number: 74-145580

Paperbound International Standard Book Number: 0-669-91199-2

Clothbound International Standard Book Number: 0-669-73304-0

To my sons,
Jonathan,
Kenneth,
Cameron and
Michael

Contents

Preface

During much of the past decade I have been studying the father-child relationship. A particular goal of my research has been to gain an understanding of paternal factors in the child's sex-role development. As a clinical psychologist I have been involved with many individuals and families seeking help, and have found that my clinical and research endeavors have cross-fertilized one another. My experiences as a son and a father, as well as a clinical and developmental psychologist, have strengthened my views about the importance of the father-child relationship.

Having had the good fortune to participate in academic and applied settings which have facilitated my research and clinical work, I have learned much from interaction with competent and sensitive colleagues, both students and faculty. In particular, I want to express my appreciation to Irving E. Alexander, Lloyd J. Borstelmann, Sheldon Cashdan, Anthony Davids, Dwight Heath, Weston La Barre, Lewis P. Lipsitt, Owen L. McConnell, David L. Singer, and James J. Stack. Some of my research has received financial support from the Public Health Service of the National Institute of Mental Health (1-F1-MH-32, 808-01; 1-R03-MH-15, 728-01).

Some of the material in this book is partially based upon my earlier attempts to integrate theory and research; parts of chapters 1, 4, and 7 are related to an article in *Developmental Psychology* (Biller, 1970); parts of Chapters 2, 3, and 5 to articles in the *Merrill-Palmer Quarterly* (Biller, 1971; Biller & Borstelmann, 1967); and parts of Chapter 6 to an article in the *Journal of Genetic Psychology* (Biller & Weiss, 1970). The editorial assistance that I have received in preparing journal articles has taught me much that was relevant in the writing of this book. I especially want to thank Boyd R. McCandless, Editor of *Developmental Psychology,* for his consistently warm encouragement and expert suggestions.

Paul H. Mussen, a general editor of Heath Lexington Books in Psychology, gave valuable comments after reading the preliminary draft. John Beck, Geoffrey Gunn, and Sid Seamans, members of the Heath Lexington Books staff, have helped make the completion of this book enjoyable and educative.

H.B.B.

1 Father-Absence and Masculine Development

In contrast to the emphasis on the mother-child relationship, there has been relatively little attention given to the impact of the father-child relationship on personality development. There is much evidence that the family in western industrial society has been matricentric, and the father's primary significance has frequently been viewed simply in terms of his ability to provide economically for his family. Throughout most of the first half of the twentieth century, child rearing was seen mainly as the mother's responsibility, and the father was not expected to be an important person in the socialization process (Gorer, 1948; Kluckhohn, 1949).

It has been assumed that men are not particularly interested in being with their children. Mothering has been considered to be a central facet of the feminine role, but fathering has not been included as an essential function of the masculine role (Benson, 1968; Nash, 1965). Although men have been viewed as heroes in many different contexts, the male in the fathering role has frequently been pictured as ineffectual (Birdwhistell, 1957; Foster, 1964). There was also a paucity of scientific inquiry into the nature and consequences of fathering until quite recently. For example, a review of American family research between 1929-1956 revealed only 11 publications pertaining to the father-child relationship but 160 concerned with the mother-child relationship (Peterson et al., 1959). The lack of recognition of the importance of the father's role was also evidenced in nineteenth century child-rearing literature in Europe and the United States (Nash, 1965; Sunley, 1955).

Much of the current interest in the father's role seems to have been intensified by the growing awareness of the prevalence of fatherless families and the social, economic, and psychological problems that such families often encounter. The fatherless family is a source of increasing concern in many industrialized countries (Wynn, 1964). More than 10 percent of the children in the United States—a total in excess of six million—live in fatherless families (Clausen, 1966; Herzog & Sudia, 1970). Fatherless families are especially common

1

among the lower class and particularly among lower-class black families, approaching fifty percent in some areas (King, 1945; Moynihan, 1965).

Many writers have speculated that the primary effects of father-absence are manifested in terms of deficits and/or abnormalities in the boy's sex-role development (e.g., Biller, 1970; Yarrow, 1964). In this chapter, research findings concerning the relationship between father-absence and the boy's sex-role development are discussed. An examination of the sex-role development of father-absent boys suggests some of the ways in which fathering can influence personality development.

Comparisons of Father-Absent and Father-Present Boys

The bulk of the early research dealing with the effects of father-absence was related to the concern for families in which the fathers were or had been absent because of military service during World War II (e.g., Bach, 1946; Sears, 1951; Stolz et al., 1954).

The Sears conducted a pioneering investigation of the effects of father-absence on three- to five-year-old children. Each child was given an opportunity to play with a standardized set of doll play equipment and the investigators recorded his behavior. Compared to the father-present boys, the father-absent boys were found to be less aggressive, and they also seemed to depict less sex-role differentiation in their doll play activity. For example, their play contained less emphasis on the maleness of the father and boy dolls (Sears, 1951; Sears, Pintler & Sears, 1946).

Bach (1946) used a similar procedure to study the effects of father-absence on six- to ten-year-old children. As in the Sears study, father-absent boys were less aggressive in doll play than were father-present boys. Bach observed that "the father-separated children produced an idealistic and feminine fantasy picture of the father when compared to the control children who elaborated the father's aggressive tendencies" (p. 79).

In Santrock's (1970a) study of four- and five-year-old disadvantaged black children, father-absent boys exhibited less masculine and more dependent behavior in standardized doll play situations than did father-present boys, although the two groups of boys did not differ in amount of aggressive behavior. In addition, maternal interviews indicated that the father-absent boys were less aggressive as well as less masculine and more dependent than the father-present boys.

In a very thorough investigation, Stolz et al. (1954) gathered data concerning four- to eight-year-old children who for approximately the first two years of their lives had been separated from their fathers. Interview results revealed that the previously father-separated boys were generally perceived by their fathers as being "sissies." Careful observation of these boys supported this view. They were less assertively aggressive and independent in their peer relations than boys who had not been separated from their fathers; they were more often observed to be very submissive or to react with immature hostility. The boys who had been father-absent were actually more aggressive in doll play than boys who had not been separated from their fathers. However, the fact that the fathers were present in the home at the time of this study, and that the father-child relationships were stressful, makes it difficult to speculate about what influence father-absence per se had on the children's personality development.

There is additional evidence that the effects of early father-absence on boys persist even after their fathers return. Carlsmith (1964) studied middle-class and upper-middle-class high school males who had experienced early father-absence because of their father's military service during World War II. Father-absence before the age of five was related to the patterning of College Board Aptitude Scores. Compared to the usual male pattern of math score higher than verbal score, the pattern of the father-absent subjects was more frequently the same as the female pattern—verbal score higher than math score. Moreover, "the relative superiority of verbal to math aptitudes increases steadily the longer the father is absent and the younger the child when the father left" (p. 10). Other researchers have also found that early father-absence is related to a feminine patterning of aptitude test scores (e.g., Altus, 1958; Nelsen & Maccoby, 1966).

Leichty (1956) compared the projective test responses of male college students who were father-absent between the ages of three to five to those of a matched group who had not been father-absent. In terms of responses to the Blacky Pictures, fewer of the father-absent students said "Blacky" would like to pattern himself after his father, more often choosing "Mother" or "Tippy," a sibling. Such a response can be conceived of as a projective indication of underlying sex-role orientation, the father-absent males being less masculine. However, it is not clear from the data Leichty presented how many of the father-absent group chose Tippy. This response might also indicate a masculine sex-role orientation if Tippy was depicted by the respondent as being a male sibling. Rabin (1958) found that fewer 9- to 11-year-old Kibbutz boys than non-Kibbutz boys said Blacky would like to pattern himself after his father. This finding is consistent with the fact that the Kibbutz boys had less contact with their fathers than did the non-Kibbutz boys. Unfortunately, as in Leichty's study, it is not evident from data presentation how many of the boys chose Tippy.

Paternal occupation can be related to frequent father-absence. In a very extensive investigation Tiller (1958) and Lynn and Sawrey (1959) studied Norwegian children aged eight to nine and a half whose fathers were sailors absent at least nine months a year. They compared these father-separated children with a matched group of children whose fathers had jobs which did not require them to be separated from their families. The boys' responses to projective tests, and interviews with their mothers, indicated that father-separation was associated with compensatory masculinity (the boys at times behaving in an exaggerated masculine manner, at other times behaving in a highly feminine manner). The father-separated boys appeared to be much less secure in their masculinity than did the control group boys. Consistent with the findings of Sears (1951) and Bach (1946), the father-separated boys were less aggressive in doll play than the control group. A difficulty in interpreting the results of the Tiller, and Lynn and Sawrey, research is the difference in sociocultural background between the father-absent and father-present families (families headed by sailor officers in contrast to those headed by businessmen and white-collar workers).

Several investigators have attempted to assess differences between father-absent and father-present boys in terms of their human figure drawings. Phelan (1964) assumed that boys who drew a female when asked to draw a person had failed to make a shift from an initial identification with the mother to an identification with the father.

In her study, there was a higher rate of father-absence among elementary-school-age boys who drew a female first as compared to those who drew a male first. An additional analysis of my (1968a) data with kindergarten-age children revealed that father-absent, as compared to father-present, boys were less likely to draw a male first or to clearly differentiate their male and female drawings. However, relationships between father-absence and figure drawings have generally not been found with older children (e.g., Domini, 1967; Lawton & Sechrest, 1962). A problem with most of the studies concerned with figure drawings is that there is no presentation of specific information regarding length and age of onset of father-absence.

Developmental Stages

Data presented by Pedersen and Rabson (1969) suggest that the father-son relationship is important even during the child's first year of life. In an intriguing attempt to explore the impact of fathering on infants, these investigators studied correlates of the infants' attachment behavior. The infants' behavior was observed at eight months and again at nine and one-half months, and mothers were interviewed regarding father-participation when the infants were nine and one-half months old. Pedersen and Rabson found that the degree to which the father participated in caretaking (e.g., giving bottles, changing diapers, etc.), engaged in stimulating play (e.g., excitatory and arousing activity), and was generally emotionally involved with his infant son was related to the infant's attachment to his father (i.e., intensity of infant's greeting behavior upon the father's return, directed smiles, vocalization, increased level of excitement). The authors speculated that such early father-son attachment may be an important factor in the sex-role development process.

Research by Money (1965) and the Hampsons (1965) has pointed to the first two to three years of life as being of crucial importance in the formation of an individual's sex-role orientation. On the basis of their clinical observations of individuals with physical-sexual incongruencies, these investigators have concluded that self-conceptions relating to sex-role appear particularly difficult to change after the second and third years of life. Their conclusions need to be bolstered by more objective and complex assessment of their subject's sex-role development, but such speculations are nevertheless very provocative. The possibility of critical periods in sex-role development is suggested by their findings; it may be that father-absence at different periods affects different dimensions of personality development.

Early father absence. Father-absence before the age of four or five appears to have a particularly profound effect on masculine development. Hetherington (1966) reported that 9- to 12-year-old father-absent boys manifested less masculine projective sex-role behavior and were rated by male recreation directors as more dependent on their peers, less aggressive, and as engaging in fewer physical contact games than were father-present boys. However, there were no consistent differences on the sex-role measures when the father-present boys were compared with boys who had become father-absent after the age of four. I found that father-absent five-year-old boys had less masculine sex-role orientations (fantasy game measure) and sex-role preferences (game choice) than did father-present boys (Biller, 1969b). Moreover, the boys who became father-absent before the age of four had significantly less masculine sex-role orientations than those who became father-absent in their fifth year. In an investigation Bahm and I conducted with junior high school boys, those who became father-absent before the age of five scored less masculine on an adjective check list measure of masculinity of self-concept than did those who were father-present (Biller & Bahm, 1971).

Other investigations also indicate that paternal deprivation during the first few years of life has much influence on personality development. A study of lower-class fifth grade boys by Santrock (1970b) revealed that boys who became father-absent before the age of two were more handicapped in terms of several dimensions of personality development than were boys who became father-absent at a later age. For example, boys who became father-absent before age two were found to be less trusting, less industrious, and to have more feelings of inferiority than boys who became father-absent between the ages of three to five. The impact of early paternal deprivation is also supported by Carlsmith's (1964) findings concerning cognitive functioning. Additional evidence is consistent with the supposition that early father-absence is associated with a heightened susceptibility to a variety of psychological problems (e.g., Blanchard & Biller, 1971; Holman, 1953). However, some data suggest that certain facets of development are particularly affected by father absence after the age of five (Herzog and Sudia, 1970).

From their cross-cultural perspective, Burton and Whiting (1961) discussed the possible differential impact of father-absence at different stages of the sex-role development process. Burton and Whiting pointed out that many societies have a "discontinuous identification process." The father is virtually excluded from contact with his young children. Supposedly, a discontinuity in identification is produced when the boy is pushed into masculine behavior sometime in preadolescence or adolescence, particularly through his experiences during initiation rites. In contrast to earlier female domination, he is suddenly under the direct control of adult males, and feminine behavior is negatively reinforced. It is assumed that the boy has to learn to repress his earlier feminine identification. Whiting, Kluckhohn, and Anthony (1958) discovered that societies with exclusive mother-son sleeping arrangements and long postpartum sex taboos were likely to have elaborate male initiation rites; Burton & Whiting hypothesized "that the initiation rites serve psychologically to brainwash the primary feminine identity and establish firmly the secondary male identity" (p. 90).

In support of their "sex-role identification conflict hypothesis," Burton and Whiting (1961) reported some rather dramatic cross-cultural evidence. In societies in which rules of residence were matrilocal and in which the infant sleeps and interacts almost exclusively with females during the first few years of his life, a custom called the *couvade* was likely to occur. This custom stipulates that the husband retire to his bed upon the birth of his offspring and act as though he had just gone through childbirth. This custom can be interpreted as symbolic of an underlying feminine identification.

Different Aspects of Sex-Role Development

As the findings relating to developmental stages have suggested, different aspects of sex-role may not be affected in the same way by father-absence. Hodges, McCandless, and Spicker found that young father-absent children intensely seek the attention of older males (McCandless, 1967). Because of such deprivation effects, father-absent children often have a strong motivation to imitate and please potential father figures (Freud and Burlingham, 1944; Mumbauer, 1969). Father-absent boys may strive to act masculine in some facets of their behavior while continuing to behave in an unmasculine or feminine manner in others.

It is important to discuss different aspects of sex-role because so much of the research concerning the father-absent boy has been focused on his apparent difficulties in sex-role development. The evaluation and integration of previous research, as well as the planning of future research, necessitates consideration of conceptual and methodological issues related to the study of sex-role development.

I have differentiated among three general aspects of sex role development: sex role *orientation,* sex role *preference,* and sex role *adoption* (Biller & Borstelmann, 1967). These distinctions are based, in part, on earlier conceptualizations of the sex-typing process (e.g., Kagan, 1964; Lynn, 1959). Sex-role orientation is considered to be one dimension of an individual's self-concept. It includes the individual's evaluation of his maleness and/or femaleness. Much of this evaluation is a product of learning experiences which take place early in the individual's life. The child becomes oriented in varying degrees toward assuming the requisites of the male or female role during his first few years of life. Parent-child interaction during this period is very crucial. The boy's perception of himself as more similar to his father than his mother appears particularly important. A young boy with an inadequate or absent father can be expected to have particular difficulty in developing a masculine sex-role orientation. As the child matures, his orientation becomes more complex and relates to his perception and evaluation of the degree to which his internal standards and overt behavior approximate general cultural as well as familial expectations. In this context, sex-role orientation seems similar to what Kagan (1964) referred to as sex-role identity.

Whereas sex-role orientation relates to an individual's perception of himself, sex-role preference is concerned with his evaluation of certain environmental opportunities. Sex-role preference refers to an individual's relative desire to adhere to the cultural prescriptions and proscriptions of the masculine and/or feminine role. The concept designates a preferential set toward symbols or representations of sex-role that are socially defined. It relates to his preferences for certain roles, activities, interests, and attitudes. Choice or discrimination is implied in such behavior, and a preference for a given role varies in strength from individual to individual. It can be predicted that lack of a paternal-role model also retards the development of a masculine sex-role preference.

In contrast to sex-role orientation and sex-role preference, sex-role adoption refers to the complex pattern of the individual's publicly observable behavior, particularly in the framework of social inter-action. An individual's sex-role adoption relates to how masculine and/or feminine members of his particular society view his behavior. Again, the presence of an adequate father would seem important. Because sex-role adoption has many facets, simply equating mascu-linity of adoption with a particular behavior such as physical aggression might lead to many errors of classification. In terms of masculinity, the degree of the individual's assertiveness, competitive-ness, independence, and activity directed toward physical prowess and mastery of his environment should be taken into account. An unmasculine adoption seems represented by behaviors such as pas-sivity, dependency, and timidity.

At this point one may ask why it is necessary to distinguish sex-role orientation from sex-role adoption, or for that matter, sex-role preference. A general consistency among these three aspects of sex-role is expected in many individuals. A masculine sex-role orientation predisposes a boy, though it does not compel him, to develop a masculine sex-role preference and sex-role adoption. However, for some individuals, early learning experiences, as compared to those in later life, are inconsistent and/or conflict-producing. For example, a paternally deprived boy may be exposed only to females who en-courage passivity and dependency in the first four or five years of his life, while later there is much peer and societal pressure for him to behave in a masculine manner. Demands for masculine behavior may not become apparent to the boy until he reaches school age or even adolescence, but in any case under such conditions his sex-role preference and/or sex-role adoption may differ from his basic sex-role orientation.

Measurement. Attention needs to be paid to ways in which different aspects of sex-role can be measured (Biller & Borstelmann, 1967). Sex-role orientation seems a necessary concept, but difficult to define and measure. The use of self-description techniques such as adjective check lists appears to be a particularly clear-cut procedure to assess self-perceptions of masculinity-femininity (e.g., Biller & Bahm, 1970; Heilbrun, 1965a). However, sex-role orientation is not easily measurable in many individuals because of their defensiveness and/or adherence to social expectations. Thus, special indirect or projective situations (such as drawings, fantasy play, and TAT-like responses) have often been used so that the individual may express sex-role inclinations which might otherwise be constrained by social and conscious self-expectations.

Assessment of an individual's human-figure drawings appears to be a possible way of evaluating his sex-role orientation. In many studies the sex of the first figure drawn has been interpreted as a measure of sex-role orientation (e.g., Biller, 1968a). But, particularly with adolescents and adults, sex of the first figure drawn is not in itself a reliable measure of sex-role orientation (Brown & Tolor, 1957). In addition to the sex of the figure drawn, it may be worthwhile to take into account specific details in drawings (e.g., Swenson & Newton, 1955). The Franck Drawing Completion Test (Franck & Rosen, 1948), is an attempt to assess the masculinity-femininity of subjects' elaborations of incomplete line figures (e.g., angles are considered masculine, curved lines feminine). This technique has been found to have some utility with adolescents and adults (e.g., Biller & Barry, 1971; Miller & Swanson, 1960).

The most widely used technique for assessing children's sex-role development has been Brown's (1956) IT Scale for Children (ITSC). In the usual procedure, the child is presented with a picture of an ambiguous child figure, "IT," and is asked to choose what "IT" would like in a series of pictures of various socially sex-typed items. In this way, Brown attempted to get at the child's sex-role inclinations in an indirect manner. A frequent criticism leveled against this technique is that "IT" actually looks more like a boy than a girl, and many children think they are supposed to make choices for a boy figure rather than "projecting" their own choices onto "IT" (Brown, 1962). Despite this, the IT Scale has been found to have considerable construct validity (e.g., Hetherington, 1966; Mussen and Rutherford, 1963).

The concept of sex-role preference calls for exposure of the individual to a choice situation in which there are relatively masculine and feminine alternatives available. Rabban (1950) constructed a choice procedure consisting of eight masculine toys and eight feminine toys, and methods for assessing sex-role preference through picture choices have been developed along similar lines (e.g., Anastasiow, 1965; Biller, 1969d). The Terman and Miles Interest Inventory and the similar masculinity-femininity scales of the Minnesota Multiphasic Personality Inventory (MMPI), Strong Vocational Interest Blank, and California Psychological Inventory (Gough Femininity Scale) seem essentially techniques to measure sex-role preference in adolescents and adults (e.g., Engel, 1967).

Inherent in most approaches to measuring sex-role preference is an assumption that masculinity and femininity are polar opposites. Supposedly, the more boys differ from girls in their sex-role preferences, the more masculine they are. Rosenberg and Sutton-Smith (1959) have developed a game preference test on which preadolescent boys and girls can be assessed on both masculinity and femininity, masculine games being those almost always selected by boys and feminine items being those almost always selected by girls. The child's preferences are compared with both same sex and opposite sex norms. With this technique, masculinity and femininity scores are not merely the reverse of one another, independently scored scales being available.

It is difficult to specify the complexity and range of behaviors that can be encompassed under the rubric of sex-role adoption. Some investigators have used simple point scale ratings of masculinity-femininity (e.g., Koch, 1956). Peer ratings have also been used (e.g., Gray, 1957), and Sears, Rau, and Alpert (1965) assessed the amount of time children spent in sex-typed play areas. Freedheim (1960) had first- to fifth-grade teachers select the boys they perceived as most and least masculine in their classes, and he was able to find out what behaviors were most characteristic of high masculine and low masculine boys. Other investigators have developed similar procedures (e.g., Biller, 1968a; Vroegh et al., 1967). There has also been an attempt to develop a rating procedure with which masculine and feminine behaviors can be rated separately (Biller & Liebman, 1971).

It is becoming increasingly evident that sex-role development is an extremely complex process. For example, as well as there being several different aspects of sex-role, each aspect of sex-role can have both a masculine and a feminine component. That is, an individual can have both masculine and feminine characteristics and assessment of his masculinity may not give a meaningful estimate of his femininity. Available data indicate that there are only low positive relationships among procedures attempting to measure different aspects of sex-role. A multidimensional approach is necessary for adequate assessment (Biller, 1968a; Biller & Borstelmann, 1967).

**Variations in the Father-Absent Boy's
Sex-Role Development**

The results of many studies can be construed as indicating that the effect of father-absence varies in terms of which aspects of sex-role are considered. D'Andrade (1962) investigated the impact of several kinds of family patterns on the sex-role development of 5- to 14-year-old children. One of his procedures can be considered to be a measure of sex-role preference. (The child was asked whether he preferred to pretend to be the father, mother, brother, or sister, if he were playing a game). In terms of this procedure, boys whose fathers had been continually absent made just about as many masculine choices as boys whose fathers had been continually present. D'Andrade also used a projective drawing completion test (Franck Test) to assess the boys' sex-role development. The number of subjects at different age levels was very small, but assessment of the completed drawings suggested that some of the boys who were without fathers during their first few years of life had unmasculine and/or feminine sex-role orientations even though most appeared quite masculine in their sex-role preferences.

Barclay and Cusumano (1967) did not find any differences between father-present and father-absent adolescent males on a measure of sex-role preference (Gough Femininity Scale). However, the father-absent males, as compared to the father-present males, were more field-dependent in terms of Witkin's rod and frame test. Barclay and

Cusumano conceptualized the field-dependence—field-independence dimension as reflecting underlying sex-role orientation, an interesting but questionable assumption.

In my (1968b) study with lower-class six-year-old children, father-absent boys were significantly less masculine than father-present boys on a measure of projective sex-role behavior (ITSC). Such a procedure can be assumed to assess sex-role orientation. However, the two groups were not consistently different in terms of their direct sex-role preferences (the toys and games they said they liked) or teachers' ratings of sex-role adoption. Results from my (1969b) study with five-year-old boys also suggested that sex-role orientation is more affected by father absence than are sex-role preference or sex-role adoption. Even though the father-absent boys had significantly less masculine game preferences than the father-present boys, differences between the groups were most clear-cut in terms of responses to the sex-role orientation procedure. No consistent differences were apparent with respect to the sex-role adoption measure. It is interesting to note that among father-present boys, the degree of both perceived father dominance and father dominance in father-mother interaction appears to be more related to measures of sex-role orientation than to measures of sex-role preference or sex-role adoption (Biller, 1969a).

Social background. If it can be assumed that more middle-class adolescents than lower-class adolescents eventually attend college, an investigation by Altus (1958) suggests that father-absent middle-class boys remain relatively low in masculinity of sex-role preference throughout adolescence. Father-absent and father-present male freshmen at the University of California were compared. Father-absence was due to divorce, but no data on the age of onset of father-absence were reported. The father-absent group scored significantly higher than the father-present group on the masculinity-femininity scale of the MMPI, indicating less masculinity of interests and attitudes.

In contrast, an examination of data from several other studies suggests the hypothesis that, particularly by adolescence, there is relatively little difference among lower-class father-present and father-absent boys with respect to many facets of sex-role awareness, preference, and adoption (Aldous, 1969; Barclay & Cusumano, 1967; Greenstein, 1966; Miller, 1961; Mitchell & Wilson, 1967; McCord, McCord & Thurber, 1962; Tiller, 1961).

Greenstein (1966) studied adolescent boys referred to a juvenile court-affiliated diagnostic center. Father-absent and father-present males were not found to be significantly different in terms of their responses to a masculinity-femininity inventory and other sex-role measures. Subjects were considered to be father-absent if, at least three years prior to age 12, no adult male was living in their home. However, at the time of the study, 10 of the 25 father-absent boys were residing in homes in which an adult male was present.

Miller (1961), with a seemingly more representative subject population, compared father-absent lower-class junior high school boys, predominantly black and Puerto Rican, with a matched group of father-present boys. There were no clear-cut differences, on either a masculinity-femininity interest inventory or in teachers' ratings of aggression and dependency. A boy was considered to be father-absent if no male lived in his home for at least two years prior to the study.

Such a short-term criteria of father-absence does not indicate in how many cases the father (or a father surrogate) was available in the preschool years, and if so, for how long. For example, paternal availability during the preschool years for the adolescent father-absent boys could account for their relatively masculine sex-role development.

McCord, McCord, and Thurber (1962) analyzed social workers' observations of predominantly lower-class 10- to 15-year-old boys. These investigators did not find any differences in the sex-appropriate behavior of boys separated from their fathers before the age of 6 and father-present boys. However, many boys separated from their fathers between the ages of 6 and 12 exhibited a feminine-aggressive pattern of behavior. A feminine-aggressive pattern of behavior can be a consequence of sex-role conflict and insecurity. It is interesting that Tiller (1958) described a somewhat similar pattern of behavior for Norwegian father-separated boys.

The masculinity of many father-absent boys may be a reflection of conflict-generated overcompensation. Father-absent boys, particularly those in the lower class, seem to have an abundance of highly masculine peers whom they can emulate. Some observers have speculated that among lower-class adolescent boys, those who are father-absent often exceed those who are father-present in certain dimensions of masculine behavior (e.g., Burton & Whiting, 1961; Miller, 1958). Terman and Miles (1936), although not describing their father-absent subjects in sufficient detail, did note that this group scored significantly above the median for males in terms of masculinity of interests. Santrock and Wohlford (1971), in their study of lower-class fifth grade boys, found that teachers rated father-absent boys as more aggressive and masculine than they did father-present boys. By late childhood lower-class father-absent boys appear to score at least as high as their father-present counterparts on certain measures of sex-role preference and sex-role adoption.

Surrogate Models

All children experience father-absence to some degree. Usually it is while the father is away at work. The father may be separated from his children for prolonged periods or permanently because of economic factors, occupation, war, desertion, divorce, hospitalization, or death. An almost infinite variety of patterns of father-absence can be specified. Many factors need to be considered in describing the father-absent situation: type (constant, intermittent, etc.), length, cause, the child's sex and age, quality of mother-child interactions, sibling constellation, and sociocultural background. The absent father can still have an ongoing psychological impact on his child. The child may have memories of past interactions and/or develop a perception of his father from what others tell him. In this way the absent father can function as a model for the child. One of Freud's and Burlingham's (1944) case studies provides a poignant illustration. Tony, a two-year-old, only lived with his family up until the age of eighteen months, and he saw his father very little. His actual relationship with his father was very limited, but Tony perceived himself as having an extremely close relationship with his father. He talked about his father doing everything with him and he attempted to emulate every detail about his father's behavior that he could remember.

Paternal absence or paternal inadequacy does not rule out the possible presence of other male models. A brother, uncle, grandfather, or male boarder may provide the boy with much adult male contact. An important role can be played by male neighbors and teachers. The child may even learn some masculine behaviors by patterning himself after a movie or television star, an athlete, or a fictional hero. Freud and Burlingham (1944) have described how a fatherless two-year-old boy developed a fantasy-role model. Bob's mother had told him about a nine-year-old boy whom he referred to as "Big Bobby" and thereafter Bob actively used Big Bobby as a masculine model, attempting physical feats that he thought Big Bobby could perform. Bob perceived Big Bobby as physically superior to everyone else.

Some investigators have found that masculinity is related to the general amount of contact boys have with adult males. Nash (1965) studied a group of Scottish orphans who went to live in cottages run by married couples, the husbands thus offering them a masculine model. Even though less masculine (in terms of a variety of sex-role measures) than boys who were raised in a typical family setting, they were more masculine than a group of orphans brought up entirely by women. In Steimel's (1960) investigation, adolescent boys who were high (compared to those who were low) in masculinity of interests on both the MMPI and Strong Vocational Interest Blank, recalled more childhood experiences with older males. In terms of maternal interview data, Santrock (1970a) found that father-absent boys with a father substitute were significantly less dependent than father-absent boys with no father substitute.

A child's relationships with his siblings can affect many facets of his personality development and in some families siblings may have more impact on a child's development than do his parents. Koch (1956) and Rosenberg and Sutton-Smith (1964) have contributed much to our understanding of sibling influences on sex-role and personality development. For example, Koch found that young boys who have older brothers are more likely to be exposed to male group influence and to exhibit masculine behaviors than are boys with older sisters. Although many complex variations have been found when different sibling constellations have been compared, there is considerable evidence indicating that boys with brothers are more masculine than boys with sisters, especially in two-child families (e.g., Brim, 1958; Rosenberg & Sutton-Smith, 1964; Sutton-Smith & Rosenberg, 1965).

In two-child father-absent families, boys with brothers seem to suffer less of a deficit in academic aptitude than do boys with sisters (Sutton-Smith, Rosenberg & Landy, 1968). Santrock (1970a) found that father-absent boys with only older male siblings scored more masculine (on a maternal interview measure of sex-role behavior) than did father-absent boys with only older female siblings. In an extension of Santrock's investigation, Wohlford et al. (1971) found that father-absent children with older brothers were less dependent than those without older brothers in terms of both doll play and maternal interview measures. However, the presence or absence of older female siblings was not related to the sex-role measures and did not affect the older brother's influence.

The presence of male siblings may lessen the effects of paternal deprivation, but data from another recent investigation were consistent with the conclusion that the presence of a father is generally a much more important factor in masculine development than is the presence of an older brother (Biller, 1968a). It is also relevant to note that the sibling constellation in a family may influence the behavior of parents as well as children. For example, there is evidence that fathers' attitudes concerning what constitutes appropriate sex-role behavior are influenced by the sex of their children (Lansky, 1967).

Peer group. Peers are very important models for masculine behavior. The masculine-role models provided by the peer group can be particularly influential for the paternally deprived boy. In a social class or subculture in which instrumental aggression and physical prowess are very important as a means of achieving peer acceptance, many father-absent boys are likely to emulate their masculine peers. Peer models seem especially significant in lower-class neighborhoods. Miller (1958) pointed to the centrality of such traits as toughness and independence in the value system of lower-class adolescents. Lower-class boys honor aggressiveness more than do middle-class boys, and one of the types of boys they most admire is the aggressive, belligerent youngster who earns their respect because of his toughness and strength (Pope, 1953).

The focus on masculine behavior in the adolescent gang provides the father-absent lower-class boy with many substitute masculine models. Miller (1958, p. 14) emphasized that:

For boys reared in female-based households the corner group provides the first real opportunity to learn essential aspects of the male role in the context of peers facing similar problems of sex-role identification.

During the elementary school years, and in some cases even earlier, peer group pressure for masculine behavior begins to have an effect on most paternally deprived boys. There are some family situations in which emotional and instrumental dependency on the mother is so strong that the tough neighborhood does not have an effect or its impact is postponed until adolescence. Because of certain physical handicaps such as lack of strength or coordination, it may be relatively impossible for a boy to successfully interact with a masculine striving peer group. On the other hand, the boy who is physically well-equipped may find it relatively easy to gain acceptance from his peers.

Summary

Comparisons of father-absent and father-present boys suggested that availability of the father is an important factor in the masculine development of young boys. There is evidence that the young father-absent boy is more dependent, less aggressive, and less competent in peer relationships than his father-present counterpart. He seems likely to have an unmasculine self-concept. However, analysis of previous investigations revealed methodological deficiencies and indicated that a number of factors must be taken into account if the impact of father-absence on masculine behavior is to be fully understood.

The first few years of life appear to be particularly important in masculine development, and father-absence during this period seems to have an especially retarding effect. If the boy becomes father-absent after the age of five, his sex-role development appears to be much less affected than if he becomes father-absent early in life. Different aspects of sex-role development are not influenced in the same way by father-absence. Sex-role orientation, that aspect of sex-role relating to self-concept, seems to be most hampered by father-absence in the first few years of life. Sex-role preference and at least some facets of sex-role adoption appear to be less influenced by father-absence.

Father-absent boys learn many masculine behaviors. Even in the father's absence, other males can play a very important role in the boy's masculine development. For example, lower-class father-absent boys usually learn many masculine behaviors from their peers and generally behave in a masculine manner, although there is evidence that they are likely to have unmasculine sex-role orientations and to behave in an overly rigid fashion.

There needs to be a systematic consideration of how such variables as age of onset of father-absence, the availability of father surrogates, sibling constellation, and peer group interactions influence different aspects of the father-absent boy's sex-role development. A general problem with studies comparing father-absent and father-present children is that investigators have usually treated both father-absent children and father-present children as if they represented homo-genious groups. There have been only a few attempts to match father-absent and father-present children on potentially important variables, such as intelligence, sociocultural background and variations in the mother-child relationship. Similarly, there has been a lack of concern for the meaning of father-absence and father-presence. For example, there has been little effort to ensure that a group of consistently father-absent boys is compared with a group of boys who have a high level of father availability.

Preview. A function of Chapter 1 is the introduction of topics which are considered in greater detail in other parts of the book. Many of the issues raised in this chapter are clarified in ensuing chapters. One of the major concerns of this book is the difficulties in the sex-role and personality development encountered by the paternally deprived child. An equally as important emphasis is on the ways in which the father-child relationship can facilitate the child's sex-role and per-sonality functioning.

Chapter 2 contains an analysis of the consequences of variations in the father-son relationship on the boy's sex-role development. There is a consideration of theories of identification and the effects of paternal masculinity, nurturance, limit-setting, and overall paternal salience. Chapter 3 includes an examination of the role of sociocultural and constitutional variables on the father-child relationship. An attempt is made to present an integrated view of the interaction of familial, constitutional, and sociocultural factors on the boy's masculine development. Chapter 4 reviews evidence concerning the influence of adequate and inadequate fathering on different facets of cognitive, emotional, and interpersonal functioning. There is considerable elaboration of the possible role of paternal deprivation and father-absence in the development of psychopathology.

Chapter 5 analyzes the impact of the mother-son relationship on the boy's personality development. There is much consideration of ways in which the mother can affect the father-absent boy's sex-role development. Chapter 5 contains material pertaining to the father-absent boy's peer group interactions and the economic and social meaning of the absence of the mother's husband. Fathering and feminine development is discussed in Chapter 6. A portion of Chapter 6 is devoted to the concept of femininity and there is also a review of data relating to the effects of father-absence on girls. Chapter 7 provides an overview of research and practical implications. Much of the discussion in Chapter 7 is relevant to the sex-role development of paternally deprived and father-absent children.

2 Father-Presence and Masculine Development

In this chapter, evidence pertaining to the impact of the father-son relationship on masculine development is reviewed. There are continuums of paternal influence on which both father-absent and father-present boys can be placed. Examination of the father-absent boy's sex-role functioning may lead to a clearer view of the impact that the father usually has in the masculine development process. In a similar way, consideration of variations in the father-son relationship in the intact home can be of heuristic value in understanding what difficulties the father-absent boy may encounter.

Identification Theory Hypotheses

Theories of identification have stimulated the major hypotheses pertaining to the boy's sex-role development. Identification theorists attempt to account for more than sex-role development and are also concerned with conscience development, impulse control, and adult role-playing behavior. In this section, hypotheses relating to the development of masculinity are discussed.

The Freudian view of the father's role in masculine development is described first, since other identification theory hypotheses are, at least in part, derivatives (Bronfenbrenner, 1960). Freud alluded to anatomical and other biological differences between the sexes as predisposing different behavior patterns, but he also believed that both males and females had bisexual characteristics. He often depicted parent-child interactions as important determinants of sex-role development (Freud, 1950; 1955). Freud postulated that the boy desires to have an exclusive relationship with his mother during the oedipal period, when he is three to five years of age. At this point, supposedly, the boy is still closely identified with his mother. Freud believed that the boy begins to perceive his father as a very aggressive competitor for his mother's affection and to fear that his father will castrate him.

Freud hypothesized that the boy's oedipal conflicts were resolved when he identified with his father, the aggressor, and repressed his desire to possess his mother. The boy's subsequent strong masculine strivings and desire to be like his father were seen as a by-product of his identification with his father. Bronfenbrenner (1960) pointed out that Freud, in his later writings, described "an identification of an affectionate sort" between the boy and his father, and that some affectionate dependency on the father may increase the probability of "identification with the aggressor." Nevertheless, in Freudian theory the perception of the father as punitive and threatening, as the "source of decisive frustrations" during the oedipal period, is the major prerequisite for the boy's masculine development (Fenichel, 1945, p. 95).

Whiting's (1959) status-envy theory of identification is an extension of the Freudian hypothesis of identification with the aggressor. Whereas the Freudian hypothesis stressed the boy's desire to possess his mother, Whiting emphasized that the child wants to engage in many of the activities of the envied parent. According to this conception, a young boy will develop masculine behavior only if his father (or a father surrogate) is the primary consumer of valued resources. For instance, Whiting argued that the boy will have a masculine identification if he perceives his father as having access to more privileges and attractive objects and activities than does his mother. It is assumed that the child is motivated to imitate the behavior of the primary recipient of valued resources and that his identification with that person is much strengthened by fantasy rehearsal of the envied behavior.

Mowrer (1950) relied on learning theory concepts in his attempt to understand the identification process. In reformulating Freudian theory, he distinguished between defensive and developmental identification. In Mowrer's terminology defensive identification is similar to the Freudian concept of identification with the aggressor. Although Mowrer acknowledged that identification with the aggressor may be involved in the masculine development process, he emphasized the importance of developmental identification. The basis for developmental identification is an affectional-emotional link with the parent which has developed out of a nurturant parent-child relationship; the child becomes dependent on the parent to provide nurturance and affection (see also Sanford, 1955; Sears, 1957; Stoke, 1950).

Mowrer claimed that such a relationship motivates the child to reproduce "bits of the beloved parent" in order to avoid the feeling of loss of love when the parent withholds nurturance and praise, or is absent. It is reasoned that the boy initially identifies with the mother, but as the father becomes more a source of reinforcement, around the age of four, the boy begins to imitate his father and to behave in a masculine manner. A major learning theory hypothesis is that masculine development is positively related to the amount of nurturance the boy receives from his father. The father's warmth and affection contributes to the amount of love and respect the boy has for his father. And it follows that the more love and respect a boy has for his father, the more reinforcing his father's approval is for him.

A view of identification which, in certain respects, combines the Freudian and learning theory hypotheses has been advanced by some sociologists (e.g., Cottrell, 1942; Parsons, 1955). According to role theory, the boy identifies with the person who is most able to dispense both rewards and punishments to him—the person who most often influences his behavior. Bronfenbrenner (1960) pointed out that the novel conception of role theory, as elaborated by Parsons, is that "the child identifies not with the parent as a total person, but with the reciprocal role relationship that is functioning for the child at a particular time" (p. 32). In other words, the boy learns to play a particular role in his interaction with his father. Parsons claimed that the boy identifies with the instrumental role of the father, and in this way the boy becomes masculine (1955; 1958). A central facet of the father's instrumental role is mastery of the environment. In terms of his functioning at home, the father's instrumental role includes decisionmaking for the family and limit-setting for the children. Similar to role theorists, social power theorists emphasize that the model who is most likely to be imitated is the one who most controls valued resources (e.g., Bandura & Walters, 1963; Kagan, 1958b; Mussen & Distler, 1959).

There are many similarities among hypotheses derived from theories of identification. The hypotheses stress the importance of the father-son relationship and the boy imitating his father, although with different emphases: Freudian theory, the father as punitive and threatening; status-envy theory, the father as the primary consumer of resources; learning theory, the father as rewarding and affectionate; role theory, the father as the principal rewarding and punitive agent;

social power theory, the father as the primary controller of resources. From each of these theories, it can be predicted that if the father were absent, or if the mother were more dominant than the father, the young boy would experience difficulties in the masculine development process. To some extent, the role and social power theory hypotheses with their stress on the father's overall significance seem to integrate the other formulations.

Paternal Masculinity

There are data which indicate that the quality of the father-son relationship is a more important influence on the boy's masculine development than the amount of time the father spends at home (Biller, 1968a). A crucial factor in the father-present boy's masculine development is the degree to which his father exhibits masculine behavior. The results of some studies suggest that there is not a direct relationship between the amount the boy imitates his father and the boy's masculinity (Hartup, 1962; Kohlberg & Zigler, 1967). Imitation of the father enhances the boy's masculine development only if the father displays masculine behavior in the presence of his son.

When the father consistently adopts a maternal-like role, it is likely that his son will be relatively low in masculinity. Bronfenbrenner (1958), reanalyzing data originally collected by Lansky (1956), found that adolescent boys low in masculinity of interests often came from homes in which the father played a traditionally feminine role. The fathers of these boys took over such activities as cooking and household chores and did not generally participate in family decisionmaking or limit-setting. Bronfenbrenner also described the findings of a study by Altucher (1957) in which adolescent boys with low masculine interests "were likely to come from families in which there was little role differentiation in household activities, and in which the mother, rather than the father, tended to dominate in the setting of limits for the child" (p. 120). What seems to inhibit the boy's masculine development is not the father's participation in some traditionally feminine activities in the home per se (e.g., helping with the housework), but the father's surrendering of the masculine role in the family (e.g., decisionmaking) and/or a relative parental role reversal.

In an investigation with elementary school children, Kagan (1958a) found that over 40 percent of the boys rated low in aggression by their teachers, as compared to only about 10 percent of those rated high in aggression, perceived their mothers "as boss at home." In Freedheim's (1960) study of second- to fifth-grade children, the degree to which boys perceived their fathers as decisionmakers was related to both the masculinity of the boys' projective sex-role behavior (ITSC toy choices) and teachers' ratings of sex-role adoption. In his research with third graders, Rutherford (1969) discovered a positive association between children's ability to perceive how masculine other children were and paternal dominance. Heilbrun's (1965b) data, based on paper and pencil tests, revealed that there was a relationship between the amount of masculinity college males attributed to themselves and to their fathers. In Rychlak and Legerski's (1967) study, most adolescent boys who viewed themselves as similar to their fathers also perceived themselves and their fathers as relatively masculine.

I have found a strong relationship between kindergarten-age boys' masculinity and the degree to which they perceived their fathers as making family decisions (Biller, 1969a). In terms of measures of sex-role orientation, sex-role preference, and sex-role adoption, a high level of perceived father-decisionmaking was associated with strongly masculine behavior. Perceived father decisionmaking was particularly highly correlated with sex-role orientation. Perceived father competence was most related to sex-role orientation, although it was also significantly related to preference and adoption.

Even though there is a consistency of findings in terms of an apparent relationship between father's and son's masculinity, the studies cited above share a common methodological shortcoming. Measurement of father and son masculinity was generally not independent, both assessments usually being deduced from the son's responses. It could be argued that such evidence is not a sufficient basis on which to conclude that father's and son's masculinity is related. For example, one alternative explanation is that masculine sons will tend to see their fathers as highly masculine regardless of their father's actual masculinity. A boy may appear similar to his father yet have learned his masculine behavior not from him but from his peer group. As Bronfenbrenner (1958) pointed out, the boy's perceived similarity to his father is not necessarily a measure of his identification with his father. Father-son similarity may be just a reflection of exposure to a common social environment.

Parental Interaction. In a methodologically superior study, Hethering-ton (1965) evaluated the relative dominance of parents by placing them in an actual decisionmaking situation. She found that masculinity of preschool-age and preadolescent boy's projective sex-role behavior (ITSC) was positively related to paternal dominance. Moreover, she has discovered a general tendency for similarity between father and son to be higher in father-dominant than in mother-dominant homes (Hetherington, 1965; Hetherington and Brackbill, 1963; Hetherington and Frankie, 1967).

Using essentially the same parental interaction procedure as Hetherington (1965), I found that father dominance in father-mother interaction was positively related to kindergarten-age boys' sex-role orientations, preferences, and adoptions (Biller, 1969a). A high degree of father dominance was related to high orientation and high prefer-ences and there was a tendency for a low degree of father dominance to be associated with low adoption. Furthermore, father dominance in father-mother interaction was related to the boy's perception of father dominance.

However, it is also important to point out that in my (1969a) study, father dominance in parental interaction showed weaker relationships with sex-role development than did the boy's perception of father dominance. The boy's behavior seems to be much deter-mined by his particular perception of family interactions and it may be that his view of the father is the most veritical measure. The boy's perception of his father can also be influenced by his mother's behavior. In father-mother interactions some mothers encouraged their husbands to make decisions while others appeared to prevent their husbands from serving as adequate models by constantly competing with them for the decisionmaking role.

Other analyses of data in the above-mentioned study suggested the complex influences of family interactions on the boy's sex-role development. Several of the boys who were low in masculinity had fathers who were dominant in terms of father-mother interaction and generally seemed masculine. However, these fathers also appeared to be controlling and restrictive of their son's behavior. For instance, this type of dominant father punished his son for disagreeing with him. Masculine development is facilitated when the father is dominant (a masculine model) *and* allows and encourages the boy to be dominant. Such paternal behavior is particularly important in sex-role adoption development. In families in which the mother and father were competing for the decisionmaking function, boys were often very restricted. It seems that in some families, when the mother does not allow her husband to be dominant, he is more apt to attempt to dominate his son in a restrictive and controlling manner. (In Chapter 5 there is a detailed discussion of the mother's role in the sex-role development process.)

Studies just discussed have dealt with assessments of the father's sex-role adoption in the family. Several researchers have not found a clear-cut relationship between fathers' and sons' sex-role preferences (Angrilli, 1960; Payne & Mussen, 1966; Mussen & Rutherford, 1963; Terman and Miles, 1936).

It could be conjectured that it is the father's sex-role adoption in family interactions that is crucial and not the degree of masculine behavior that he exhibits outside the home. Many fathers have masculine interests and are masculine in their peer and work relationships, but are very ineffectual in their interactions with their wives and children. The stereotype of the masculine hardworking father whose primary activity at home is lying on the couch, watching television, or sleeping, is an all too accurate description of many fathers. If the boy's father is not consistently involved in family functioning, it is much harder for his son to learn to be appropriately assertive, active, aggressive, and independent.

Paternal Nurturance

In a study with elementary school age children, Bronson (1959) reported findings which indicated that both the father's masculinity and the quality of the father-son relationship have to be taken into account. Assessment of the father's behavior and the father-child relationship was based on interviews with the fathers and family history data. The masculinity of toy preferences of boys who had chronically stressful relationships with their fathers was negatively associated with the fathers' masculinity. Boys who had fathers who were undemonstrative, frustrating, and critical seemed to reject their fathers as models. In contrast, where the father-son relationship was non-stressful (father warm, affectionate, and supportive), the masculinity of boys' toy preferences was positively correlated to fathers' masculinity. Masculine development seems to be facilitated when the father is both masculine and nurturant.

There is other evidence in line with the learning theory contention that a warm, affectionate father-son relationship can facilitate the boy's masculine development. In a study by Pauline Sears (1953), preschool boys who assumed the father role in doll play activities tended to have warm, affectionate fathers. Mussen and Distler (1959) studied the structured doll play of kindergarten boys. Their results revealed that boys who scored high in masculinity of projective sex-role responses (ITSC) perceived fathers as more warm and nurturant than did boys with low masculinity scores. Using the same methodology, Mussen & Rutherford (1963) reported similar findings for first grade boys. Studying kindergarten-age boys, I observed that perceived father nurturance was positively related to a fantasy-game measure assessing masculinity of sex-role orientation (Biller, 1969a).

According to maternal interview data collected by Mussen and Distler (1960), the high masculine boys described in their earlier (1959) article had more affectionate relationships with their fathers than did the low masculine boys. Interviews with the boys' mothers also indicated a trend for the fathers of the high masculine boys to take care of their sons more often, as well as to have more responsibility for family child-rearing practices. Sears, Rau, and Alpert (1965) did not find interview measures of fathers' nurturance and warmth related to preschool boys' masculinity. But they did find that preschool boys' masculinity was negatively related to fathers' sex anxiety; and fathers' sex anxiety in turn was negatively associated with the amount of time that fathers participated in the infant caretaking of their sons. Fathers who are anxious about sex seem to have doubts concerning their adequacy as males. Paternal nurturance facilitates the boy's sex role development when the father is comfortable with his masculine role.

Researchers have also found that paternal nurturance is related to adolescent boys' masculinity and similarity to their fathers. In Payne and Mussen's (1956) study, boys who made similar responses to their fathers on the California Psychological Inventory depicted fathers as rewarding and affectionate on a story completion task, and, in addition, had high masculinity scores. (However, the assessments of paternal similarity and masculinity were both derived from responses to the California Psychological Inventory and were not methodologically independent.) Bandura and Walters (1959) detected an association between the degree to which adolescent males viewed their fathers as warm and affectionate and saw themselves as similar to their fathers. In Bronson's (1959) investigation, preadolescent boys who had fathers who were warm, affectionate, and supportive, tended to tell TAT stories which suggested a strong masculine sex-role orientation. Mussen (1961) found that adolescent boys with masculine interests (Strong Vocational Interest Blank) described fathers in their TAT stories as more rewarding and positive in father-son interaction than did boys with unmasculine interests. In a questionnaire study with college students, Distler (1964) found a significant relationship between perceived paternal nurturance and the masculinity of the subjects' self-descriptions.

Investigations with adolescent males have provided findings indicating that general personality adjustment, as well as sex-role functioning, is enhanced by a positive father-son relationship. Mussen (1961) found that in addition to having more masculine interests, adolescents who regarded their fathers as warm and affectionate were emotionally more stable and mature than adolescents who reported little positive involvement with their fathers. Heilbrun's (1962) data suggested that adolescents who perceived themselves as being unlike their fathers were anxious, feminine, socially immature, and lacking in self-confidence. (There is a fuller description of evidence linking the father-son relationship to various facets of personality functioning in Chapter 4.)

Paternal Limit-Setting

Findings suggesting a relationship between paternal limit-setting and masculine development have been presented by several researchers. Lefkowitz (1962) differentiated between elementary school boys who had exclusively masculine preferences and those who made one or more feminine choices. Boys who had consistently masculine preferences had fathers who were more active in setting limits for them. In Altucher's (1957) study, more adolescent boys who scored high in masculinity, as compared to boys who scored low, said their fathers set limits for them. Moulton et al. (1966) reported similar results with male college students, but Distler (1964) did not.

In Levin and Sears (1956) study, kindergarten boys whose fathers were the principal agents of punishment manifested high levels of doll play aggression. Maternal limit-setting was found to be associated with low aggression among the elementary school boys in Kagan's (1958a) study. Results from a series of studies revealed that third grade boys who were punished for aggression at home by both their mothers and fathers were more aggressive in school than boys punished only by their mothers (Eron et al., 1963).

The implication of such data is that boys often learn to be aggressive and masculine by modeling themselves after their fathers, the disciplinary situation being particularly relevant. However, other factors may be operating to produce a relationship between paternal limit-setting and boys' aggressive behavior. Boys may be aggressive as a function of the frustration engendered by severe paternal punitiveness. Furthermore, global ratings of aggression and other complex personality traits should be viewed with some degree of caution. For example, all forms of aggression are not appropriate for boys; assertiveness in play and an active physical stance in interactions with peers seem appropriate, while tattling on other children and fighting with girls seem inappropriate (e.g., Biller and Borstelmann, 1967; Shortell & Biller, 1970).

In any case, findings concerning the influence of paternal limit-setting are inconsistent. In Mussen and Distler's (1959) study, the kindergarten boys who manifested highly masculine projective sex-role responses perceived their fathers as somewhat more punitive and threatening in structured doll play situations than did boys low in masculinity. Mussen and Rutherford (1963) found a similar trend for first grade boys. But in both studies, perceived nurturance of father was found to be much more related to high masculine preferences. In addition, Mussen and Distler (1960) ascertained nothing to indicate that the fathers of the high masculine kindergarten boys punished them more than did the fathers of the low masculine boys. In my (1969a) study with kindergarten-age boys, perceived paternal limit-setting was slightly related to a measure of sex-role orientation, but not to measures of sex-role preference or sex-role adoption. Sears, Rau, and Alpert (1965) did not find a consistent relationship between interview measures of paternal limit-setting and preschool boys' masculinity.

In Mussen's (1961) study, the adolescent boys with high masculine interests perceived their fathers as nonpunitive and nonrestrictive in their TAT stories. Some of the discrepancy between this study and the Mussen and Distler (1959) and Mussen and Rutherford (1963) studies may be due to age differences. For example, by adolescence, a father who earlier was perceived as threatening because of his "awesome size" may be less threatening when his son becomes similar in size and strength. During adolescence, the father is also less likely to use physical means of punishment and more likely to set limits verbally. A related point is that limit-setting is not necessarily performed in a punitive context.

Paternal nurturance facilitates masculine development to a greater degree than does paternal punitiveness, which is more consistent with the learning theory hypothesis than with the Freudian theory hypothesis. Nevertheless, it should be noted that the Freudian hypothesis stressed paternal punitiveness during the oedipal period, and data suggesting that highly masculine adolescent boys do not perceive their fathers as punitive are not necessarily inconsistent with such a viewpoint.

When the father plays a significant part in setting limits, the boy's masculine development is facilitated *only* if there is an already established affectionate father-son relationship. If the father is not nurturant, and is punitive, the boy will display a low level of father-imitation. Data from a study by Bandura and Walters (1959) seem particularly relevant. Adolescent boys who had highly punitive but generally nonnurturant and nonrewarding fathers exhibited relatively low father-preference and little perception of themselves as acting and thinking like their fathers.

Paternal Power

Mussen and Distler (1959) found that boys with highly masculine projective sex-role behavior perceived their fathers as more 'powerful' than did boys low in masculinity. When perceived nurturance and perceived punitiveness scores were combined, the difference between the masculine and nonmasculine boys was particularly clear-cut. Mussen and Rutherford (1963) reported similar results for first grade boys, but the relationship was not as strong.

Freedheim's (1960) findings also point to the importance of the total pattern of the father-son relationship (Freedheim & Borstelmann, 1963). Second to fifth grade boys' perceptions of their fathers' decisionmaking, nurturance, and limit-setting were assessed in a structured interview. Perceived salience of the father was defined as the median percent of the time the boy played with the father doll in making up doll play stories. Paternal decisionmaking and salience were related to both masculinity of projective sex-role behavior (ITSC toy selection items) and sex-role adoption (teachers' ratings). The combination of paternal decisionmaking and salience related highest to both measures of masculinity. Though neither paternal nurturance nor limit-setting was significantly related to the measures of masculinity, when combined, they were related.

In my (1969a) investigation, as in the other studies just described, the role theory and the social power theory hypotheses seemed to be supported more than other identification theory hypotheses. In that study, the overall amount of perceived father influence was more important than perception of the father as dominant in a particular area. In addition, experiments concerning the imitation process in young children have added evidence for the role theory and social power theory formulations (e.g., Bandura, Ross & Ross, 1963; Bandura & Walters, 1963).

Parent perception and sex-role research with college students has also yielded results which are in line with formulations stressing the importance of the total father-son relationship. In Winch's (1962) questionnaire study, college males who had been separated from their fathers continually from before ten years of age, perceived their mothers as both more nurturant and controlling than their fathers, and also tended to see themselves as less similar to their fathers than did college males who had not been separated from their fathers. Distler (1964) found that those college males who described themselves as most masculine on an adjective check list viewed their fathers as high in nurturance, limit-setting, and competence; in other words, as very powerful. In Moulton et al.'s (1966) study, college males with the most appropriate sex-typing (modified version of Gough's Femininity Scale) reported that their fathers were high in affection and the dominant disciplinarians in their families. It is also interesting to note that Bronfenbrenner's (1961) findings suggested that the development of leadership, responsibility, and social maturity in adolescent males is closely associated with a father-son relationship which is not only nurturant, but includes a strong component of paternal limit-setting.

Summary

The major hypotheses concerning the father's role in the masculine development process stem from theories of identification. A discussion of these hypotheses suggests that the role theory and social power theory formulations, with their emphasis on the father's overall influence, integrate important facets of the other identification theory hypotheses.

There are data which indicate that paternal masculinity, paternal nurturance, and paternal limit-setting can be important factors in the masculine development process. However, taken separately, not one of these factors is sufficient to ensure that the boy will become masculine. A boy can have a masculine father who is not very involved in his family. His father can be nurturant but not be very effective as a masculine model. The father can be very masculine and limit-setting yet not have developed a basic affectionate relationship with his son.

A warm relationship with a father who is himself secure in his masculinity is a crucial factor in the boy's masculine development. Boys who have punitive, rejecting fathers or passive, ineffectual fathers generally have less adequate sex-role functioning than do boys who have interested-nurturant fathers who play a salient and decisive role in family interactions.

Having a father does not guarantee that the boy's sex-role development will go smoothly. To put it another way, all father-present boys do not become masculine. On the other hand, in Chapter 1 it is pointed out that many father-absent boys develop masculine behavior patterns. Future studies should compare father-absent boys with boys who have highly available and involved fathers, as well as with boys who have fathers who are relatively unavailable and/or ineffectual. It can be predicted that boys with highly available and salient fathers are, as a group, more securely masculine than either father-absent boys or boys who have ineffectual fathers. It can also be predicted that father-present boys with ineffectual fathers are not more masculine (and may even be less masculine) than father-absent boys. An examination of data presented in my (1968a) paper supports such predictions, but more research is needed.

A shortcoming of most of the studies discussed in this chapter is that data sources were not independent. In many of the studies both the father-child relationship and the son's sex-role development were assessed from the boy's responses. In other studies, information about the father-child relationship was gathered from maternal reports. Fathers should be included in data assessment. More direct observation of father-child interaction is needed if the father's impact on the child's personality development is to be better understood.

3

Paternal Influence — Sociocultural and Constitutional Factors

The impact of fathering cannot be considered in isolation from the family's sociocultural milieu and the child's constitutional characteristics. Social class differences, cultural expectations regarding sex differences, and constitutional variables are discussed in this chapter. This material, along with data and speculations introduced in the first two chapters, serves to set the stage for a multidimensional conception of masculine development.

Socioeconomic Status

One basis for the father's power and esteem is his ability to economically provide for his family. Fathers who have low-status occupations are more apt to be viewed in a negative way than are fathers with relatively high-status occupations. If the wife has a higher occupational status than her husband, marital conflict and problems in child rearing seem particularly likely to occur (Gover, 1963; Roth & Peck, 1951).

Fathers in lower-class families often appear to make attempts to dominate their families and support a patriarchal view of the family, but they frequently have very little actual influence in the decision-making process. Even though fathers in middle-class families seem to be less concerned with having absolute authority in family interactions, they appear to exert more influence (Blood & Wolfe, 1960). Lower-class fathers seem to be more punitive but less affectionate than middle-class fathers (McKinley, 1964). It has been found that the father is perceived as a less powerful figure in lower-class families than in middle-class families. For example, adolescents in lower-class families, compared to those in middle-class families, are more likely to perceive their mothers as more dominant than their fathers (e.g. Bowerman & Elder, 1964; Distler, 1964).

In light of the findings discussed in Chapter 2, it might be speculated that lower-class boys experience more difficulties in their relationships with their fathers and in their sex-role development

35

than do middle-class boys. However, even though middle-class fathers may be potentially powerful models for their sons, there is other evidence which suggests that they are frequently not very involved with their children.

Paternal availability is related to social class. The relative lack of father-participation, as vividly pictured by Green (1946) in his description of the uninvolved middle-class commuting father, interferes with the boy's masculine development. In Rabban's (1950) study, working-class boys made exclusively sex appropriate toy choices earlier than did middle-class boys (at five years as compared to six years). Rabban noted that many of the middle-class fathers in his sample were away from home a great deal, ostensibly because of occupational demands, and seemed to interact very little with their sons.

Hall and Keith (1964) found that lower-class boys had more masculine IT scores than did middle-class boys, but other investigators have failed to find social class differences on the IT Scale (e.g., Brown, 1957; Hartup & Zook, 1960). In reviewing their data, Hartup and Zook (1960) speculated that the reason for not finding social class differences was that more than half of their lower-class group did not have fathers living at home. The incidence of continual father-absence is highest in the lower-class (Miller, 1958; Rainwater & Yancey, 1967). Father-absence among lower-class families may cancel out potential differences in masculinity between lower-class and middle-class preschool-age boys, at least in terms of some measures of sex-role.

It often seems that when researchers describe lower-class fathers as patriarchal, they are referring to individuals who have relatively stable blue-collar occupations (e.g., teamsters, skilled factory workers). Of course, the operational definition of lower class may differ from study to study, but general social class distinctions are meaningful. Comparisons among lower-class (disadvantaged groups), working-class, middle-class, and upper-class families may be particularly useful in examining variations in fathering.

Among the lower class, and in some segments of the middle class, there are high rates of father-absence although the patterns differ. In the lower class, prolonged father-absence because of divorce, desertion, or separation is more common than in the working or middle class. In the middle class, especially the upper middle class, the father's occupational requirements and interests may severely limit his participation in the child-rearing process. On the other hand, Davis and Havighurst (1946), in their study of class differences in child-rearing practices, found that lower-class fathers spent less time with their children than did middle-class fathers. Lower-class fathers spent less time with their children in such activities as taking walks, as well as in educational functions.

Paternal occupation. Numerous investigators have also suggested that the type of work in which a father engages can influence the personality development of his children (e.g., Gold & Slater, 1958; Miller & Swanson, 1958). For example, Miller and Swanson speculated that fathers who are entrepreneurs, those who take risks and individual responsibility in their business ventures, encourage the development of self-control, self-reliance, and assertive mastery of the environment. According to Miller and Swanson, fathers who are engaged in bureaucratic occupations take few risks and encourage more conformity behavior in their children. There is some evidence that fathers with entrepreneurial occupations are more likely to be dominant family decisionmakers than are fathers with bureaucratic occupations (Gold & Slater, 1958). However, as Benson (1968) pointed out, many studies do not support conceptualizations which predict a direct relationship between fathers' occupations and the personality development of children.

Even in our highly mobile society, the boy's career choice is often very much influenced by his father's occupation (Mussen, Conger & Kagan, 1969). Boys whose fathers are involved in a profession or a skilled trade are apt to choose the same or a similar occupation. Nevertheless, the quality of the father-child relationship is much more important than the father's specific occupation. For example, boys who are highly identified with their fathers seem to be particularly likely to be interested in entering masculine-type occupations (Crites, 1962).

Certainly, the father in his work role can provide an important model for his son, but the amount of opportunity the son has to interact and observe his father is the critical variable. Fathers in many different occupations often have very little to do with their children. If the quality of the father-child relationship were taken into account, more clear-cut findings pertaining to relationships among paternal occupation and personality development might be forthcoming.

Cultural Expectations

The father's role, as well as expectations for male and female behavior, vary somewhat from society to society, indicating the modifiability of human behavior through learning. There are some interesting examples which stand in contrast to our society.

Among the Marquesans, men commonly engage in many activities relating to cooking, housekeeping, and child care (Linton, 1936). Other dramatic descriptions of societies which have much different conceptions of sex differences than does our society have been provided by Mead (1935). Nevertheless, there is much similarity among different societies in terms of what activities are designated as sex appropriate. Murdock (1936) studied sex-role differentiation in 224 societies and concluded that women usually engaged in more sedentary and domestic activities such as housework, cooking, and child care, whereas men were usually responsible for hunting, fishing, and other more strenuous activities relating to the support of the family.

Barry, Bacon, and Child (1957) found that a majority of societies expect and socialize their boys to be more self-reliant and achievement-oriented than girls, and their girls to be more nurturant and responsible than boys. In most cases, girls are taught how to care for children, whereas boys learn how to master their physical environment and to function independently. Zelditch (1955), examined data from 56 societies. He concluded that the father's role was primarily of an instrumental nature in 48 of the societies, and the mother's role, expressive in 50 of the societies. Mothers in most societies are the experts in interpersonal relations whereas fathers are more able to help their families in terms of solving environmental problems.

Societies differ tremendously with respect to the usual amount of time the father is available to his child. Romney's (1965) reanalysis of Barry, Bacon, and Child's (1957) findings indicates that, in societies where there is relatively little father availability, emphasis on children being compliant prevails; whereas in societies with high father availability, children are expected to be assertive. Romney's data can be interpreted as suggesting that in societies in which there is high father availability, individuals are more likely to actualize their individual potentialities. It can also be speculated that children are better adjusted in societies in which the father is actively involved in child rearing. Bacon, Child, and Barry (1963) discovered that societies with relatively low father availability have a higher rate of crime than do societies in which the father is relatively available. Stephens' (1962) data suggest that intense, restrictive mother-child relationships are more likely to occur in societies in which there is relatively low father availability in childhood. Close binding mother-child relationships appear to be negatively related to sexual adjustment in adulthood. The findings from these studies are discussed in more detail in subsequent chapters.

Sex differences. Even though our society is less differentiated in terms of sex typing than are many economically underdeveloped nations, socialization practices in the United States foster quite clear-cut sex differences. Such sex differences are precursors to the differential functioning of mothers and fathers in terms of instrumental and expressive roles.

Boys are generally expected to be, and are, more physically competent, aggressive, competitive, independent, and dominant; girls more skillful in verbal communication, nurturant, submissive, passive, dependent, polite, tactful, and neat. Peer group play and imitation of parental activities provide the opportunity to learn sex-typed behavior. Boys generally choose to participate in activities of a mechanical nature, such as building model racing cars, and games in which speed, strength, and aggression are strongly rewarded, such as contact sports. Girls prefer more sedentary and domestic activities, such as playing house and working in the kitchen (e.g., Biller & Borstelmann, 1967; Garai & Scheinfeld, 1969; Kagan, 1964).

Sex differences in the play behavior of year-old infants have been observed (Goldberg & Lewis, 1969), and some differences between the toy preferences of boys and girls in the second year of life have been reported (Benjamin, 1932). By the age of three or four, many boys are making predominantly masculine choices (e.g., Hartup & Zook, 1960). By the age of four or five, most children are aware that their parents expect them to prefer sex-typed activities (e.g., Fauls & Smith, 1956). By the age of eight or nine most boys make almost exclusively masculine choices in highly stereotyped situations (Brown,

1957), although there seem to be greater variations with more subtle measures (Rosenberg & Sutton-Smith, 1959). In any case boys' sex-role preferences seem to be more clear-cut than girls' sex-role preferences (e.g., Brown, 1957; Rosenberg & Sutton-Smith, 1960). Consistent with a general preference for the male role over the female role, typically masculine games appear to have more prestige value among children (e.g., Brown, 1958; Lynn, 1959).

In our society there is more pressure for boys to conform to masculine standards than for girls to conform to feminine standards. Boys also seem to be more concerned with, and aware of, inappropriate sex-role behavior than are girls. Tomboys are much more tolerated than "sissies." Males seem to have more adjustment difficulties in childhood, but by adulthood there appears to be less of a sex difference in the incidence of psychological problems (Lynn, 1961). It is also interesting to note that our society seems to be more permissive in terms of what girls may do during childhood but that boys appear to have more freedom to deviate from certain sex-typed activities in adulthood. For example, girls can play many masculine games in childhood yet are pressured into a quite circumscribed feminine role in adulthood.

Most children learn to perceive themselves as more similar to their same sex than to their opposite sex parent (e.g., Emmerich, 1959). However, girls seem to be more influenced by their family relationships than do boys and to imitate their mothers more than boys imitate their fathers (Duhamel & Biller, 1969; Gray & Klaus, 1956; Hartup, 1962; Sears Rau & Alpert, 1965).

According to Lynn (1969), the girl has the opportunity to learn the female role and its details from her mother while the boy must actively determine how to be masculine, since his father is not available often enough to help him learn the specifics of the masculine role. Unfortunately, many boys have little opportunity to learn that being a father requires involvement and is rewarding. Learning how to be a mother is considered to be a central part of the feminine role, but the process of learning how to be an adequate father is often ignored.

Although children generally perceive their fathers as stronger and as more competent, they usually view them as less understanding and as more punitive than their mothers. They see their mothers as friendlier and warmer and are more likely to fear their fathers. They are more often critical of their fathers, and they appear to communicate more adequately with their mothers than they do with their fathers (e.g., Benson, 1968; Goldin, 1969).

Such findings suggest that boys are more likely to have difficulties in their sex-role development than are girls. Boys have more difficulty in school than do girls and are more often labeled as emotionally disturbed or delinquent (Lynn, 1961). However, constitutionally related sex differences stemming from genetic and prenatal factors may, to some extent, account for boys' more frequent problems in impulse control and school achievement (e.g., Bronfenbrenner, 1967).

Constitutional Variables

La Barre (1954) emphasized the difference between living in a male body as compared to a female body. In addition to genital and reproductive system differences, there are other constitutional sex differences even in infancy (Garai & Scheinfeld, 1968). For example, male infants are, on the average, larger in every dimension, more muscular (Garn, 1958), more active (Knop, 1946), and have higher pain thresholds than female infants (Lipsitt & Levy, 1959). Whether or not they have more energy at their disposal, boys have higher basal metabolism rates than girls, suggesting that they "live faster" (Garn & Clark, 1953). Differences among members of the same sex as well as between sexes would also seem to be predisposed by variations in hormone functioning (Hamburg & Lunde, 1966).

Both the mother and father are influenced by constitutionally predisposed differences in their children. However, there is evidence suggesting that fathers are more concerned with sex differences than are mothers (Biller & Weiss, 1970), and it can be predicted that fathers are also more influenced by sex-role related constitutional variations in their children. Fathers' interactions with their children may be especially influenced in terms of how closely the children's physical and behavioral characteristics approximate sex-role norms.

Fathering a male infant who is strong and active is very rewarding for most men. However, if a male infant is relatively fragile and listless, his father may be less likely to perceive him in a positive manner. Similarly, a female infant who is attractive and responsive to affection may elicit different paternal behavior than the female infant who is unattractive and unresponsive.

Constitutionally influenced characteristics, including the boy's physique and related factors such as strength, stamina, and coordination, are associated with parent-and-peer expectations for masculine behavior, as well as being important determinants of the boy's success in masculine activities. Sheldon's (1944) research suggested very strong relationships between a mesomorphic physique and masculine behavior and subsequent investigations, though reporting lesser relationships, are consistent with his findings (e.g., Mussen & Jones, 1957; Seltzer, 1948; Walker, 1962, 1963).

Fathers are less tolerant of intellectually handicapped children than are mothers (Farber, 1962). They appear to be particularly upset when the retarded child is a boy. Mental retardation often leads to difficulties in sex-role development but it is likely that paternal rejection as well as a lesser learning capacity is involved (Biller & Borstelmann, 1965). The issue is very complex, for, as is discussed in Chapter 4, paternal deprivation also seems to contribute to difficulties in intellectual functioning.

The teaching of complex skills to children is often a significant part of fathering. But when the child is intellectually or physically handicapped, the task may appear impossible, especially to the father who has had little experience in patiently interacting with young children. The father who highly values intellectual accomplishment, is particularly apt to reject a retarded child (Downey, 1963). In a similar way, the father who considers physical competance as very important is likely to reject a child who is frail and/or poorly coordinated.

It is often very difficult to determine whether the child's constitutional predispositions or the father's ability to interact with his child is most influential. In any case, it is important to take both the father's and child's characteristics into consideration. For example, the father's age and physical status can be important determinants of the father-son relationship. A father who is old and/or sick may be severely limited in interacting with his child. However, a father who is physically or intellectually handicapped may have more empathy for a child who is developmentally retarded.

A Multidimensional Conception of
Masculine Development

In this section, there is an attempt to present an integrated description of masculine development which takes into account the interaction of constitutional, sociocultural, and familial variables.

As is discussed in Chapter 2, the role and social power theory hypotheses concerning masculine development appear the most consistent with empirical data, although the other identification theory hypotheses gain some support. The formulation to be presented here is partially based on social learning theory as elaborated by Bandura and Walters (1963; Mischel, 1966). Although Bandura and Walters outlined no explicit theory of masculine development, assuming all behaviors to be learned by essentially the same process, their stress on imitation is particularly relevant for an understanding of the influence of fathering on masculine development (Biller, 1968a; Biller and Borstelmann, 1967). However, the effects of cognitive and constitutional factors are also emphasized in the present formulation.

The most influential identification theories provide very interesting hypotheses concerning masculine development. However, these hypotheses generally do not take constitutional and/or sociocultural factors into account, and most of them seem to set the initial learning of specifically masculine behavior quite late in the child's development. Furthermore, these formulations are not intricate enough to consider all the factors contributing to the different aspects and patterns of sex-role development.

Sex role orientation. For many children, the development of sex-role orientation, an important facet of self concept, begins in the latter part of the first year of life. The period between one and three years appears especially important in such learning. The boy's perception of himself as a male and thus more similar to his father than to his mother, is an impetus for the boy to imitate his father. Discrimination between initial concepts of male and female usually develops by the third year of life, and with increasing age, the basis on which the child can discriminate between male and female broadens (Brown, 1958; Kagan, 1958b). Parents, by such verbal cues as "just like your daddy," facilitate their son's perception of similarity to his father, and through imitation of the father, the boy increasingly sees himself as more similar to his father. Kagan (1958b) emphasized the significance of the child's perceived similarity to the parent of the same sex, both as a motive to imitate, and as a reinforcement in the sense that the more the child imitates him, the more he perceives himself as similar. Continuing imitation of the father helps strengthen the boy's conception of himself as a male.

An examination of the evidence concerning constitutionally based sex differences leads to the expectation that children will more often resemble their same sex than their opposite sex parents. Fathers and sons can be very similar as a result of a common genetic inheritance. Even if the father is absent or ineffectual, the boy may appear to be much like his father. For example, his activity level, degree of emotional responsiveness, and physical characteristics may closely approximate his father's and make it easy for his mother to generalize that he and his father are similar in many other ways. The boy can receive much reinforcement for approximating his absent father's behavior. The mother's evaluation of the father can have much positive or negative influence on the boy's perception of himself. Of course, in terms of certain constitutional predispositions, the child from birth can more closely resemble his opposite sex parent. For example, the boy's facial characteristics, complexion, and temperment may be more like his mother's than his father's. This may make it very difficult for him to perceive himself as similar to his father. If the boy is father-absent, or has an ineffectual father, problems in sex-role development are even more likely to arise.

An important factor in the development of a masculine orientation is the availability of the father, or another significant older male, as a discriminable male object. If the boy is to develop a positive masculine self-concept, he must receive consistent nurturance and positive feedback. Contrary to the supposition of most identification theorists, even in the first two years of life, many boys develop firm attachments to their fathers. It is not justified to assume that all boys have an initial feminine identification with their mothers which they must later unlearn or repress.

Paternal nurturance facilitates the development of a masculine orientation, but the father's (or another older male's) availability seems the key condition. The mother may be relatively more nurturant than the father, but only if a masculine father is particularly frustrating or rejecting would consistent paternal availability be a detrimental factor. In such a situation, the boy might defensively align himself with his mother against his father and see himself as unlike his father.

Kohlberg's (1966) cognitive-developmental conception of sex-role development is especially relevant in discussing the development of sex-role orientation. Kohlberg placed much needed emphasis on cognitive influences which, for the most part, have been ignored in identification theory hypotheses. He proposed that sex-role development is a facet of the general process of cognitive development and, thus, accompanies the child's growing awareness of physical and social reality. Following this view, children first discover that they are either boys or girls, and on this basis they form appropriate sex-role preferences which, in turn, lead to identification with their same sex parent. According to Kohlberg, parent-child relationships are relatively unimportant. Supposedly, they are only influential to the extent that they provide a warm environment encouraging the trying out of appropriate sex-role behaviors or, on the other hand, a cold hostile milieu inhibiting adequate sex-role learning.

There are many similarities between Kohlberg's conception of sex-role development and the present formulation; the early learning of orientation, the importance of cognitive factors, the predisposing influence of orientation on later sex-role development, and the influence of self-concept and competency motivation. However, the present formulation is much more inclusive. Kohlberg gave a somewhat circumscribed description of sex-role development. He seemed to assume that knowledge of sex-role is isomorphic with sex-role development. Even though the ability to discriminate masculine and feminine roles, symbols, and activities is an important factor in sex-role development, it does not encompass all of sex-role development. There are many individuals who have knowledge of sex-role norms but prefer to behave in an opposite sex manner. For example, a boy can be aware that he is a male and possess knowledge about sex-typed toys yet prefer to play with girls' toys.

Sex-role preference. The development of an individual's sex-role preference, his relative desire to adhere to culturally defined sex-role guidelines is usually influenced by his sex-role orientation. But whereas *orientation* is very much related to discrimination between the specific sex-role models of mother and father, *preference* pertains to discrimination between more general, socially defined symbols and representations of sex-role. Sex-role orientation is involved with the individual's evaluation of himself; sex-role preference is related to the individual's evaluation of certain environmental activities and opportunities. In developing a masculine sex-role preference, the boy learns to value certain toys, activities, and interests. Learning experiences are based on more than family interactions. Peers and the mass media become increasingly influential.

But knowledge of social sex-role distinctions is not sufficient for the development of a masculine preference. Variations in family interactions can be very important. In a situation in which there is a close parent-child relationship and parents do not value traditional sex-typed activities, their son's sex-role preference will probably be relatively unmasculine. For example, if his parents do not approve of strenuous physical endeavors, regarding them as dangerous, the preschool-age boy will not desire to participate in such activities, unless he learns to value them from other sources. As his peer group interactions become more influential, he may, of course, become less comfortable conforming with parental expectations.

Even though a masculine orientation generally predisposes a masculine preference, some boys have high masculine orientations but low masculine preferences. Since rather complex discrimination learning is often involved in the development of a consistent preference, a generally limiting factor may be the child's intelligence. For example, retarded children are developmentally slower forming clear-cut sex-role preferences (Biller & Borstelmann, 1965). A boy could also develop a high masculine orientation and a low masculine preference if his father were present for just his first few years of life and his mother did not expect or encourage his choice of masculine activities. Another possibility is that a father may be very nurturant and involved with his son but disapprove of traditional masculine activities.

In contrast, a boy who has a low masculine orientation can develop a high masculine preference. This type of sex-role development is most likely to occur if the father is absent or an ineffectual model, but the mother encourages and expects the boy to participate in masculine activities. (Much of Chapter 5 is devoted to a discussion of the mother's role in the paternally deprived boy's personality development.)

Sex-role adoption. Sex-role adoption is the third aspect of sex-role to be considered. Sex-role adoption refers to the masculinity and/or femininity of the individual's publicly observable behavior. Whereas sex-role orientation is related to the individual's view of himself, sex-role adoption pertains to the way in which the individual is perceived by other members of his society. Correlates of sex-role adoption are present even in early infancy and sex-role adoption continues to evolve in adolescence and adulthood, during which time interpersonal skill development in heterosexual relationships is particularly important. However, the third through fifth years of life appear to be a very significant period for sex-role adoption development. Imitation of masculine models is very important. The development of a masculine sex-role adoption, especially in the preschool years, is related to imitation of the father. A young boy's masculinity is positively related to the degree to which his father is available and behaves in a masculine manner (decisionmaking, competence, etc.) in his interaction with his family. Male siblings and peers can, of course, also be quite influential.

Paternal masculinity is very related to what White (1960) has subsumed under the heading of competency. Much of the boy's desire to imitate his father and become masculine appears to be associated with a desire to master his physical environment. For example, the boy's ability to solve problems and to build and repair various objects can be much increased if he has the frequent opportunity to observe and imitate his father.

Assuming that the father is relatively masculine, paternal nurturance facilitates the boy's masculine development. A nurturant father compared to a nonnurturant father, more frequently rewards his son's approach responses—and thus provides more opportunities for his son to observe and imitate his behavior. To put it another way, a nurturant father is a more available model than a nonnurturant father. The nurturant father's behavior is more often associated with affection and praise and it acquires more reward value. Thus, a boy with a nurturant father has more incentive to imitate his father than does a boy with a nonnurturant father. Moreover, a nurturant father seems more likely to reinforce his son for imitating him.

If the father is a frequent participant in setting limits for his son, other opportunities for imitation are provided. However, if the father is much more punitive and frustrating than rewarding, his behavior will not have a high incentive value and will be less reproduced. A positive relationship between paternal limit-setting and the masculinity of the boy's sex-role adoption can be predicted only if the father is relatively nurturant. To the extent that limit-setting is a function of the father's masculine role in the family, it would seem to be positively related to paternal decisionmaking.

Frequent paternal decisionmaking, competence, nurturance, and limit-setting can function to make the father more distinguishable from the mother and also enhance the boy's overall masculine development. The father's masculinity, nurturance, and limit-setting add to his total salience for his son. The boy's perception of his father strongly influences his perception of the incentive value of the masculine role, and all aspects of his sex role development.

Individual differences. A boy can have a masculine orientation and preference but be limited in the development of a masculine adoption by an inadequate or inappropriate physical status. A boy who is very short or very thin would seem to be at a disadvantage. Height and muscle mass seem positively related to masculinity of sex-role adoption. Though a particular type of physique is not sufficient to produce masculine behavior, a boy who is tall and broad or broad though short (mesomorphic) is better suited for success in most masculine activities than a boy who is tall and thin (ectomorphic) or short and thin. Parents and others seem to expect more masculine behavior from tall, broad, and/or mesomorphic boys.

The boy's physical status can influence his sex-role orientation and sex-role preference as well as his sex-role adoption. For example, during adolescence boys with especially unmasculine physiques are apt to have insecure self-concepts. Even though they are also likely to be low in masculinity of sex-role adoption, they may express very masculine sex-role preferences in an effort to convince themselves and others that they are masculine (Biller & Liebman, 1971). In an effort to bolster their feelings of adequacy, many adolescent boys with insecure sex role orientations engage in body-building and weight-lifting (Harlow, 1951).

The boy who has a sensory-motor handicap or is intellectually limited can be extremely frustrating to his father. For example, a very sportsminded father might find it very difficult to interact with a poorly coordinated son. Similarly, an intellectually striving father may be uninterested in spending time with a son who possesses little intellectual ability. There is some evidence which suggests that fathers are more likely to reject retarded sons than retarded daughters (Farber, 1962; Tallman, 1965).

The child's constitutional predispositions have much to do with his personality development. It is probable that a boy with a meso-morphic physique, high activity level, superior intelligence, and good coordination will be perceived as masculine and attain much success in many male activities. Even without an adequate father, such a boy can develop a strong sense of masculinity. It would take a very re-strictive and dominating mother to severely hamper his success in peer group activities. It is interesting to note that many highly success-ful athletes have come from father-absent homes. Anecdotal evidence suggests that these men were not restricted by their mothers and found a number of older men who encouraged them in the develop-ment of their skills. Older males often respond positively to a boy who possesses exceptional physical abilities. In turn, the boy who is paternally deprived is often seeking the companionship of an older male.

The influence of older males on the father-absent boy can, of course, be negative as well as positive. For example, in their search for male role models, many lower-class paternally deprived boys have formed relationships with criminals. The boy with a superior physical endowment can use his skills in antisocial activities as well as in socially approved ways. It is interesting to note that the Gluecks found that both father-absence and mesomorphic physiques were more frequent among delinquents than among nondelinquents (Glueck & Glueck, 1950; 1956).

Patterns of Sex-Role Development

At several points in this book, the advantages of examining the ante-cedents and correlates of different aspects of sex-role are stressed.

Miller and Swanson (1960) put forth the related idea of the importance of delineating the antecedents and correlates of patterns of sex-role development, and I have elaborated upon this point of view (Biller & Borstelmann, 1967). The sex-role pattern approach takes into consideration an individual's status on two or more aspects of sex role and can lead to a clearer understanding of personality functioning.

For example, there may be a discrepancy between an individual's basic sex-role orientation and his sex-role preference. By dividing measures of sex-role orientation and sex-role preference at the median, four different groups can be identified: A group with masculine orientations and masculine preferences; a group with masculine orientations and feminine preferences; a group with feminine orientations and masculine preferences; and a group with both feminine orientations and feminine preferences.

Previous research has revealed the importance of such orientation-preference patterns in terms of several areas of personality functioning. Miller and Swanson (1960) reported that variations in defensive styles and emotional reactivity were associated with particular sex-role patterns. Lipsitt and Strodbeck (1967) presented evidence indicating that an individual's sex-role pattern was related to his perception and value judgments of others. Some data suggested that level of verbal creativity in kindergarten-age boys is associated with sex-role patterns (Biller, Singer, & Fullerton, 1969). In a study with college males, individuals who were consistently masculine appeared to be more similar to their fathers and to have more adequate personality adjustments than did those with other sex-role patterns (Biller & Barry, 1971).

The studies just mentioned assessed just two aspects of sex-role. By considering three aspects of sex-role and dealing only in terms of high (H) or low (L) masculinity in each aspect, eight possible patterns can be specified. The eight patterns can be symbolized as: HHH, HHL, HLH, HLL, LHH, LHL, LLH, and LLL. If an orientation, preference, adoption ordering is used, HHH indicates that an individual has a high masculine orientation, high masculine preference, and high masculine adoption; LLL that the individual is low in masculinity in all three aspects of sex-role.

The relative frequency of particular patterns seems to be a function of the age range sampled. For example, the HLL pattern may be relatively frequent at two years, because many boys do not yet have the cognitive capacity to discriminate between culturally sex-typed symbols of sex-role or the general physical ability to imitate their fathers extensively. On the other hand, since a masculine orientation facilitates the development of a masculine preference and adoption, the HHL pattern would probably be quite rare among preadolescents.

It is also meaningful to consider the relative stability of each aspect of sex role. All three aspects of sex role can be influenced by the child's experiences. However, a child's orientation, being formed earliest in life, and being a basic dimension of his self-concept, seems more resistent to change than the other aspects of sex role. A child's sex-role preference and sex-role adoption seem to be more influenced by specific situational factors than does his sex-role orientation.

In most children, because of the converging accumulation of predisposing factors, a fair degree of consistency among the aspects of sex role can be expected, at least by their late elementary school years. A masculine orientation facilitates the development of a masculine preference; a masculine orientation and preference increase the probability of the development of a masculine adoption. Similar antecedent factors operate to produce masculinity in different aspects of behavior. For instance, the presence of an appropriate model is important for the development of both orientation and adoption. Many individuals have HHH and LLL patterns because of such consistencies in the sex-role development process.

A boy is most likely to develop an HHH pattern if his father is highly available, nurturant, and masculine. The LLL patterns seems probable if the father is absent or ineffectual, and the mother is very dominating and overprotective. Interaction with an extremely frustrating and rejecting father might also lead a boy to completely reject the masculine role.

Other sex-role patterns occur with less frequency than the HHH and LLL patterns. A boy can develop an LHH pattern as a compensatory reaction. For example, many boys with quite unmasculine orientations, in an effort to gain peer group acceptance, behave in an exaggerated masculine manner. Their rigidity is often expressed intellectually, emotionally, and socially. The LHH pattern is particularly common among boys in neighborhoods in which there is both a high incidence of paternal deprivation and an emphasis on toughness and strength. Incongruity between sex-role orientation and other aspects of sex role can lead to very high levels of anxiety and/or defensiveness.

Several sets of circumstances can promote the development of an HHL pattern. If a boy is without a masculine model after age two or three, even though he has already developed a masculine orientation and preference, it may be difficult for him to develop a masculine adoption. A boy might develop an HHL pattern if his parents encourage a masculine preference and his father is very nurturant but not masculine. In such a situation, the boy could have a masculine orientation and preference but not have a masculine model to imitate. The development of an HHL pattern might also occur if the boy has a masculine orientation and preference but a very unmasculine physique, or a physical disability which hampers his masculine role performance.

A boy could develop an LHL pattern if his father were regularly absent or ineffectual and his mother expected and encouraged a masculine preference. Assuming that he lacked an available masculine model, he might not develop a masculine orientation or adoption.

The LLH, HLH, and HLL sex-role patterns appear to be relatively infrequent; the LLH pattern because a masculine orientation and preference are usually precursors of a masculine adoption, and the HLH and HLL because a masculine orientation usually leads to the development of a masculine preference. A boy can develop an LLH pattern if he has a very aggressive, assertive mother who encourages him to behave in a similar fashion, and a father who has been consistently ineffectual. A mesomorphic physique and related characteristics might add to the probability of his developing an LLH pattern. Some active male homosexuals approximate the LLH pattern.

If a boy was cognitively retarded and thus handicapped in developing a high masculine preference, but had very encouraging and appropriately sex-typed parents, and was physically well-equipped, he might develop an HLH sex-role pattern. A physically handicapped and intellectually retarded boy might develop a masculine orientation and an HLL pattern if his father were very involved in interacting with him.

Research which is reviewed in the first two chapters is consistent with a multidimensional conception of masculine development. But much more data is needed if the development of sex-role patterns is to be understood. It must be emphasized that discussion of just three aspects of sex role, considering only high or low masculinity on each aspect, grossly oversimplifies the sex-role development process. For example, attention must be given to feminine development because individuals can have both masculine and feminine components in their orientations, preferences, and adoptions. Furthermore, there are different dimensions of each aspect of sex-role that can be analyzed.

Summary

It is important to consider sociocultural and constitutional variables when evaluating the impact of fathering. It is clear that both parents and children are influenced by their socioeconomic status and general cultural expectations. The father's occupation may be a factor in how, and the degree to which, he interacts with his son. There is still much emphasis on sex differences in our society, and the pressure for boys to conform to the masculine role is particularly strong. However, boys may experience sex-role problems because models of masculine behavior are not readily accessible to them. Among both lower- and middle-class families, lack of father availability is common, although the reasons may differ.

The father's perception of his son and his motivation to interact with him are influenced by the boy's appearance and capabilities. For example, if the boy is constitutionally predisposed to have a high level of intellectual and physical ability, it appears more likely that the father will meaningfully interact with him. In contrast, the boy who is physically or intellectually handicapped is more likely to experience paternal rejection. On the other hand, paternal deprivation can also contribute to difficulties in intellectual and social development (see especially Chapter 4).

A multidimensional formulation is necessary to clarify the complexity of sex-role development. Much emphasis must be placed on the importance of imitation of masculine models, but consideration should also be given to maternal, sociocultural, constitutional, and cognitive variables. Patternings of sex-role orientation, sex-role preference, and sex-role adoption (as well as their possible antecedents) must be differentiated if the masculine development process is to be better understood.

4

Paternal Influence and General Personality Functioning

In this chapter there is an examination of how the quality of the father-son relationship, and father-absence, may be associated with cognitive and interpersonal development. Much evidence is reviewed which indicates the way in which a positive father-child relationship can foster the development of the boy's intellectual and social skills. Many of the inadequately fathered boy's psychological handicaps can be viewed as being in varying degrees related to sex-role problems.

Cognitive Functioning

The quality of the father-son relationship in the intact home influences academic achievement as well as sex-role development. There are many paternally deprived boys who possess the necessary intellectual ability but not the self-confidence and determination to succeed academically. Kimball (1952) studied very intelligent adolescent boys who were enrolled in a residential preparatory school. She compared the underachieving boys with a group of boys randomly selected from the total school population. In terms of sentence completion test responses, significantly more of the boys in the underachieving group appeared to have poor relationships with their fathers.

Grunebaum et al. (1962) did an interesting clinical investigation concerning underachieving elementary school boys. They examined the family life of boys who had at least average intelligence, but scored one to two years below expectation on standard achievement tests. The fathers of the underachieving boys were reported to feel generally inadequate and to consider themselves failures. The fathers did not seem to offer their sons adequate models of male competence. Most of the fathers viewed their wives as being superior to them and their wives generally shared this perception. There was evidence that the mothers were involved in undermining both their husbands' and sons' feelings of adequacy.

55

Shaw and White (1965) searched for familial antecedents of academic performance in their investigation with high school students having above-average intelligence. Parents and children were administered adjective check list forms on which they were supposed to describe themselves and other members of their family. Boys who had a B average or better perceived themselves as more similar to their fathers in terms of adjective check list responses than did boys with a below B average. High-achieving boys perceived themselves as significantly more similar to their fathers than their mothers, but low-achieving boys did not. Father and son self-ratings were correlated in the high-achieving group, but not in the low-achieving group.

Mutimer, Loughlin, and Powell (1966) found that a group of boys who did well in reading were more father-identified than a group of boys who did poorly. In Anastasiow's (1965) study with young boys, those who had clear-cut masculine sex-role preferences were viewed by their teachers as being more able to enter the first grade, and also developed better reading skills than those with unmasculine sex-role preferences. If he has at least average intellectual ability, a boy who has a positive relationship with his father and is secure in his masculinity seems likely to do well in school.

Such data do not prove that lack of a positive father-son relationship hinders a boy's academic achievement. It could be argued that, in some cases, disappointment in the son's performance leads the father to reject him. The son's poor performance can further weaken an already flimsy father-son relationship. On the other hand, a father may be much more accepting and nurturant if his son performs well in school.

Genetic factors can, of course, play an important role in the degree to which the father influences his son's cognitive development. Father and son can demonstrate intellectual abilities in the same area primarily as a function of a similar genetic inheritance. In a study of college freshmen and their fathers, Poffenberger and Norton (1959) found that fathers' and sons' attitudes toward mathematics were similar, yet were not related to closeness of the father-son relationship. Poffenberger and Norton speculated that genetic factors are related to degree of success in mathematics and can predispose similar attitudes towards mathematics. However, Hill's (1967) findings suggested that more than genetic factors are involved. In Hill's study, paternal expectations proved to be associated with upper middle class seventh grade boys' attitudes toward mathematics. Boys who had positive attitudes tended to have fathers who viewed mathematics as masculine and expected their sons to be masculine.

Father availability. Many investigators have found that the father-absent child often suffers from intellectual deficits. In a study involving Scottish children, Sutherland (1930) noted that those who were father-absent scored significantly lower on an intelligence test than did those who were father-present. Sutton-Smith, Rosenberg, and Landy (1968) found that males who became father-absent early in life were more likely to have lower college aptitude scores than were males whose fathers had not been absent.

Maxwell (1961) administered the WISC to a large group of 8- to 13-year-old children referred to a British psychiatric clinic and reported that children whose fathers had been absent since the age of five performed below the norms for their age group on a number of subtests. Some of the data suggested that these father-absent children were limited in their social knowledge, but deficits in the perception of details and verbal skills also appeared to be frequent. It should be noted that father-absence since the age of five was the only background variable which consistently differentiated these children from the WISC norms, although it seems surprising that father absence before age five had no apparent effect on cognitive functioning.

Paternal deprivation is often a significant factor in the complex and debilitating process of cultural deprivation (Bronfenbrenner, 1967). Lower-class father-absent black children appear to be particularly hampered in their cognitive functioning. Investigators have found that among lower-class black children, those who are father-absent score lower on intelligence and achievement tests than do those who are father-present (Deutsch, 1960; Deutsch & Brown, 1964).

Taking into account such findings, Kohlberg (1966) has reasoned that differences in the sex-role development of father-absent and father-present boys are related to the less mature cognitive functioning of the father-absent child. Kohlberg viewed the learning of socially defined concepts of sex-role as the primary ingredient of the sex-role development process and argued that many young father-absent boys lack certain types of cognitive experience, retarding both their intellectual and sex-role development. According to Kohlberg, if father-absent and father-present boys are matched in intelligence, differences in sex-role development would not be found or would be very small. He described the data of one of his students (C. Smith) which suggest that differences between father-absent and father-present boys' sex-role preferences are considerably lessened if intellectual level is controlled. Kohlberg also emphasized that father-absent boys have the opportunity to learn more about social norms when they enter school and that, as they get older, their sex-role functioning becomes more similar to that of father-present boys. (There is a more complete discussion of Kohlberg's formulations concerning sex-role development in Chapter 3).

Father-absent children, at least after they reach school age, are not particularly deficient in their general knowledge of social norms concerning sex-typing (e.g., Biller, 1968b; Thomes, 1968). Nevertheless, the ability to discriminate between male and female attributes and activities is not sufficient to promote appropriate sex-role development. In a study with lower-class six-year-old boys, I observed that, although they were aware of the differences between male and female alternatives, father-absent boys were more likely to have unmasculine sex-role orientations than were father-present boys (Biller, 1968b). A later study with kindergarten boys indicated that father-absent boys had less masculine sex-role orientations and sex-role preferences than did father-present boys, even though the two groups were matched in terms of IQ (Biller, 1969b). Also, matching for IQ in a study with junior high school students, we found that boys who became father-absent before the age of five had less masculine self-concepts than father-present boys (Biller & Bahm, 1971). Sex-role development involves much more than the learning of social norms.

Blanchard and I (1971) assessed the effects of different levels of father-availability on the academic functioning of third-grade boys. In that investigation, we explored both the impact of father-absence and the degree of father-son interaction in the father-present home. The boys in this study were of average intelligence and were from working-class and lower-middle-class backgrounds. Four groups of boys were studied; early father-absent (beginning before age five), late father-absent (beginning after age five), low father-present (less than six hours per week), and high father-present (more than two hours per day). Subject matching across the four groups was done in terms of age, IQ, socioeconomic status, and sibling constellation. Class grades and academic achievement test scores were examined, and it was found that the academic performance of the high father-present group was much superior to the other three groups. The early father-absent boys were generally underachievers, the late father-absent and low-father-present boys usually functioned somewhat below grade level, but the high father-present group performed almost a year above grade level.

Boys from high father-present families are more likely to actualize their intellectual potential than are boys from families in which the father is absent or relatively unavailable. Highly available fathers can be models of perseverance and achievement motivation. The father can be an example of a male successfully functioning outside of the home atmosphere. Frequent opportunity to observe and imitate an adequate father contributes to the development of the boy's overall instrumental and problem solving ability. However, having a competent father will not facilitate a boy's intellectual development if the father is not consistently accessible to the boy, or if the father-son relationship is negative in quality (e.g., if the father is generally critical and frustrating).

When the father has intellectual interests, a positive father-son relationship particularly stimulates the boy's academic achievement. If the father's work involves cognitive tasks such as reading, writing, or mathematics, it is likely that the boy will develop skills in these areas. Frequent exposure to a father who enjoys intellectual activities can do much to further a child's cognitive development. However, if the father does not enjoy such activities, the child is less likely to excel in school.

Cognitive styles. The sex-typed nature of different intellectual abilities and cognitive styles is supported by the wealth of evidence concerning sex differences in intellectual functioning (Garai & Scheinfeld, 1968; Maccoby, 1966). Such skills as analytical, mathematical, spatial, and mechanical reasoning are generally viewed as more appropriate for males; and males generally do better on tasks requiring these skills than do females. On the other hand, females are superior to males in most types of verbal and communication skills. The development of certain cognitive abilities, as well as a secure sex-role, are generally facilitated by frequent interaction with a nurturant, masculine father.

Carlsmith (1964) found that middle-class high school boys who were father-absent in their early childhood were more likely, than boys who were father-present, to have a feminine patterning of aptitude test scores (see also Chapter 1). In contrast to the usual male pattern of math score higher than verbal score, boys who had been father-absent were more apt to have a higher verbal than math score. Carlsmith speculated that such a score pattern was a reflection of an unanalytical, global conceptual style. The incidence of feminine patterning was positively related to the length of father-absence and negatively related to the child's age at the onset of father-absence.

In an intriguing investigation emphasizing the complexity of the familial correlates of cognitive development, Nelsen and Maccoby (1966) also reported that early father-absence was related to the feminine patterning of aptitude test scores. Maccoby and Rau (1962) found that boys with this type of cognitive pattern were more likely to have been father-absent during early childhood, and less likely to have had a close relationship with their fathers when they were home. In addition, they were most often disciplined by their mothers.

Barclay and Cusumano's (1967) data point to difficulties in analytical functioning being associated with father-absence. Using Witkin's rod and frame procedure, these investigators found that, among adolescent males, those who were father-absent were more field-dependent than those who were father-present. Field dependence relates to an inability to ignore irrelevant environmental cues in the analysis of certain types of problems. Bieri's (1960) study revealed that boys who perceived themselves as more similar to their mothers, and as having a closer relationship with their mothers than their fathers, had difficulty with an embedded figures test—supposedly an indication of their field dependence. Dyk and Witkin (1965) reported that field-independent boys were more likely to perceive warm father-son relationships in their TAT stories than were field-dependent boys.

Dyk and Witkin also described the results of a study by Judith Seder (1957). Seder found that fathers of field-independent boys participated more actively with their sons than did fathers of field-dependent boys. Father-son participation in sports, outings, and trips was more common for the field-independent boys. Fathers of field-dependent boys spent relatively little time with their sons. Boys who have neglecting or passive fathers more often adopt a global rather than an analytical cognitive style (Witkin, 1960).

Lynn (1969), in a thought-provoking analysis, hypothesized that there is a curvilinear relationship between paternal availability and field independence. There are relatively clear-cut findings indicating that low father availability inhibits the development of field independence. However, Lynn speculated that moderate father-availability is most conducive to the development of field independence. According to Lynn, in this situation the boy has an outline of the masculine role but has to actively interact with his environment to develop his masculinity. Lynn argued that if the father is constantly available to his son, the boy will find the task of becoming masculine very easy but will not develop an analytical, independent stance in interacting with his environment.

In order to support his contention, Lynn discussed studies done with Eskimo children (Berry, 1966; MacArthur, 1967). Eskimo boys spend a great deal of time with their fathers and there is evidence that, from an early age, they engage in much imitation of the father. Interestingly, among Eskimo children, boys are not more field independent than girls. Lynn also cited a study by Sherman and Smith (1967). These investigators found that orphans who received full-time care from male counselors were less field-independent than males from normal families.

It must be pointed out that availability of a father or father surrogate is not sufficient to promote masculine-type behavior. In fact, there are some data which indicate that fathers who are constantly home often play rather unmasculine roles in their families (Biller, 1968a). When fathers or father surrogates have full-time responsibilities for the care of the child, they may take over many traditional feminine activities. Lynn noted that the male caretakers of the orphan boys in the Sherman and Smith (1967) study performed many typically mothering functions. Unless the father's or father surrogate's behavior has a clear masculine component, it will not, in itself, facilitate the boy's masculine development. It may be that there is relatively little differentiation between adult male and female Eskimos. In any case, Lynn's analysis is interesting, but much research indicates that there is a generally positive relationship between the adequacy of the boy's masculine development and the amount of interaction he has with a salient, competent father.

Social Class. Although Carlsmith (1964) did not report separate comparisons of verbal and mathematical aptitudes, it appears that the father-absent group tended to be equal or superior in verbal aptitude— though inferior in mathematical aptitude. Because academic achievement in most fields is so heavily dependent on verbal ability, father-absent *middle-class* children do not seem to be very handicapped. There are data which indicate that the middle-class mother may strongly influence the father-absent boy's intellectual functioning. Hilgard, Neuman, and Fisk (1960) studied university-affiliated families in which the father had died. They found that men who had lost their fathers during childhood tended to be highly successful in their academic pursuits despite, or maybe because of, a conspicuous overdependence on their mothers. Clinical findings presented by Gregory (1965b) suggest that many upper-middle-class students who have been father-absent do well in college, and evidence reviewed by Nelsen and Maccoby (1966) reveals that high verbal ability in boys is often associated with a close and restrictive mother-son relationship. Levy (1943) found that middle-class maternally overprotected boys also did superior work in school, particularly in subjects requiring verbal facility. However, their performance in mathematics was not at such a high level, which seems consistent with Carlsmith's conclusions.

There are other data suggesting that father-absence does not necessarily hinder intellectual functioning. Albert (1969), in a family background analysis, discovered a high rate of father loss during childhood among geniuses. He speculated that the early loss of a parent may permit the gifted individual to more freely explore his environment, and develop more original and creative types of behavior. It could also be conjectured that the intellectual development of many geniuses is facilitated by the formation of an intense relationship with an intellectually oriented mother. The childhood of Leonardo da Vinci may be an example (Freud, 1947).

In homes in which the father is absent or relatively unavailable, the mother seems to assume a more primary role in terms of dispensing reinforcements and emphasizing certain values. In fact, a father-absent boy who is strongly identified with an intellectually oriented mother has an advantage in certain facets of school adjustment. He usually finds the transition from home to the typically feminine oriented classroom quite comfortable. Such father-absent boys often do particularly well in tasks where verbal skills and conformity are rewarded. (The influence of the mother-child relationship on the father-absent boy's personality development is discussed in the next chapter.)

In future studies concerning academic performance, it would be interesting to systematically take into account the effects of both the quality of the mother-son relationship and the father-son relationship. Another intriguing area of research would be to examine the influence of parent-child interaction on academic performance as a function of sex of child as well as sex of parent. Other research could be in the direction of examining the effects of sex of teacher on the father-absent child. Young father-absent children are particularly responsive to adult males, and an appropriately behaving male teacher can do much to raise the academic performance of father-absent boys.

Variations in fathering and father-absence can have much impact on the child's cognitive development. But it must be emphasized that fathering, or the lack of it, is only one of many factors that can affect the child's intellectual development. Maternal and peer group values are particularly important. For example, among children in the lower class, father-absence usually intensifies lack of exposure to experiences linking intellectual activities with masculine interests. Many boys, in their intense efforts to view themselves as totally masculine, perceive intellectual tasks and school in general as feminine. When the school presents women as authority figures and makes strong demands for obedience and conformity, it is particularly antithetical to such boys' desperate attempts to feel masculine.

Impulsive and Antisocial Behavior

Mischel conducted a series of studies concerning the antecedents and correlates of impulse control in Caribbean children (e.g., Mischel, 1961c). In an early phase of his research, Mischel (1958) discovered that 7- to 9-year-old black West Indian children chose immediate gratification significantly more frequently than did white West Indian children. The differences between the black and white children appeared to be related to the greater incidence of father absence among the black children. Studying 8- and 9-year-olds, Mischel (1961c) found that father-absent children showed a stronger preference for immediate gratification than did father-present children. Father-absent children, for instance, more often chose a small candy bar for immediate consumption rather than waiting a week for a large candy bar. The paternally deprived child usually has less opportunity to observe adult models exercise self-control.

Mischel (1958) speculated that father-absence interferes with the young child's development of trust of other people. It is also possible that many young father-absent children trust adult females but not adult males; in Mischel's research an adult male offered the choice between immediate and delayed gratification. The young father-absent child may learn to be secure in the presence of his mother and generalize this trust to other females, but a basis for trusting adult males may be lacking.

When Mischel (1961c) studied 11- to 14-year-olds, he did not find an association between father absence and preference for immediate gratification. Perhaps, as Mischel suggested, as the father absent child grows older, his wider experience helps him to develop a trust of others beyond those in his immediate family. With added experience most father-absent children may learn to trust males. In addition, according to Mischel, many of the older father-absent children may have been without their fathers for a relatively brief period. The older paternally deprived children may have been father-present during the age period most crucial to the development of trust. In Mischel's studies, the criterion of father-absence was simply whether or not the father was living at home and there was no measure of duration of father-absence. In research with fifth-grade boys, Santrock (1970b) found that father-absence beginning in the first two years of life was more disruptive to the development of trust than father-absence during the ages of three to five.

Self-control. Whiting (1959) hypothesized that paternal deprivation is negatively related to the strength of the child's conscience development. Doing a cross-cultural analysis, he assumed that self-blame for illness is an indication of strong conscience development. In societies in which fathers have little contact with their young children, there is more of a tendency to blame others and/or supernatural beings for one's illness. Blaming one's self for illness was strongest in nuclear households and least in polygamous mother-child households. Such evidence is also consistent with the view that paternal deprivation can inhibit the development of trust in others.

Hoffman (1971) reported data concerning the conscience development of seventh-grade children. Father-absent boys consistently scored lower than father-present boys on a variety of moral indexes. They scored lower on measures of internal moral judgement, guilt following transgressions, acceptance of blame, moral values, and rule-conformity. In addition, they were rated as higher in aggression by their teachers which may also reflect difficulties in self-control. Although the influence was less clear-cut, weak father identification among father-present boys was also related to less adequate conscience development. Father identification was determined by responses to questions involving the person the boy felt most similar to, most admired, and most wanted to resemble when he grew up. Boys with strong father identifications scored higher on the measures of internal moral judgement, moral values, and conformity to rules than did boys with low father identifications.

A number of clinicians including Aichorn (1935) and Lederer (1964) have speculated about inadequacies in the conscience development of the father-absent boy. In his experience as a psychotherapist, Meerloo (1956) found that a lack of accurate time perception is also common among father-absent children. Meerloo assumed that the father represents social order and that his adherence to time schedules gives the child an important lesson in social functioning. The paternally deprived boy may find it very difficult to follow the rules of society. Antisocial acts are often impulsive as well as aggressive, and there is evidence that inability to delay gratification is associated with inaccurate time perception, lack of social responsibility, low achievement motivation, and juvenile delinquency (e.g., Mischel, 1961a, 1961b).

The father-absent boy may lack a model from whom to learn to delay gratification and to control his aggressive and destructive impulses. A boy who has experienced paternal deprivation may have particular difficulty in respecting and communicating with adult males in positions of authority. There is some evidence that perceived similarity to father is related to positive relationships with authority figures (Bieri & Lobeck, 1959). The boy whose father has set limits for him—in a nurturant and realistic manner—is better able to set limits for himself. Investigators have found that boys who receive appropriate and consistent discipline from their fathers are less likely to commit delinquent acts even if they are gang members (Glueck and Glueck, 1950; Stanfield, 1966).

Delinquency. Juvenile delinquency can have many different etiologies, but paternal deprivation is a frequent contributing factor. Many researchers have noted that father-absence is more common among delinquent boys than among nondelinquent boys. Studying adolescents, Glueck and Glueck (1950) reported that more than two-fifths of the delinquent boys were father-absent as compared with less than one-fourth of a matched nondelinquent group. McCord, McCord, and Thurber (1962) found that the lower-class father-absent boys in their study committed more felonies than did the father-present group, although the rates of gang delinquency were not different. Gregory (1965a) referred to a large number of investigations linking father-absence with delinquent behavior and also detected a strong association between these variables in his study of high school students.

Siegman (1966) analyzed medical students' responses to a questionnaire concerning their childhood experiences. He compared the responses of students who had been without a father for at least one year during their first four years of life, with those of students who had been continuously father-present. The father absent group admitted to a greater degree of antisocial behavior during childhood. Other researchers relying on self-report procedures have also reported that individuals from fatherless families are more likely to engage in delinquent behavior (Nye, 1958; Slocum & Stone, 1963). Anderson (1968) found that a history of paternal-absence was much more frequent among boys committed to a training school. He discovered that father-absent nondelinquents had a much higher rate of father-substitution (step-father, father-surrogate, etc.) between the ages of four to seven than did father-absent delinquents.

Miller (1958) argued that most lower-class boys suffer from paternal deprivation and that their antisocial behavior is often an attempt to prove that they are masculine. Bacon, Child, and Barry (1963), in a cross-cultural study, found that father availability was negatively related to the amount of theft and personal crime. Degree of father availability was defined in terms of family structure. Societies with a predominantly monogamous nuclear family structure tended to be rated low in the amount of theft and personal crime, whereas societies with a polygamous mother-child family structure tended to be rated high in both theft and personal crime. Following Miller's hypothesis, Bacon, Child, and Barry suggested that such antisocial behavior was a reaction against a female-based household and an attempted assertion of masculinity. A large number of psychiatric referrals with the complaint of aggressive acting-out are made by mothers of preadolescent and adolescent father-absent boys and clinical data suggest that sex-role conflicts are frequent in such boys (e.g., MacDonald, 1938; Wylie & Delgado, 1959).

Herzog and Sudia (1970) carefully analyzed the methodological defects of studies concerning father absence and delinquency. They pointed out that socioeconomic and sociocultural factors are often not taken into account in comparisons of father-absent and father-present children. Furthermore, Herzog and Sudia emphasized that law enforcement officials and other community agents may react differently when a father-absent child, rather than a father-present child, behaves in an antisocial manner, especially when the child comes from an economically disadvantaged family. For example, they may expect the father-absent child to commit increasingly serious offenses and he may be dealt with more severely. Such treatment may influence the father-absent child's self-concept and strengthen the probability that he will become involved in more antisocial acts.

The difficulty that boys from father-absent homes often have in relating to male authority figures can also contribute to the reactions of law enforcement officials. The father-absent boy's "lack of respect" can lead to negative interactions with male authority figures. In fact, some data suggest that father-absent boys are more prone to commit offenses against authority than against property (Herzog & Sudia, 1970; Nye, 1958).

Herzog and Sudia (1970) also referred to much evidence indicating that lack of general family cohesiveness and supervision, rather than father absence per se, is the most significant factor associated with juvenile delinquency. Many familial and non-familial factors have to be considered, and in only some cases is father absence linked to delinquent behavior. For example, boys in father-absent families who have a positive relationship with their mothers seem to be less likely to become delinquent than boys in father-present families who have inadequate fathers.

Father-present juvenile delinquents appear to have very poor relationships with their fathers. Bach and Bremer (1947) reported that preadolescent delinquent boys produced significantly fewer father fantasies on projective tests than did a nondelinquent control group. The delinquents portrayed fathers as lacking in affection and empathy. Similarly, Andry (1962) found that delinquents character-ized their fathers as glum, uncommunicative, and as employing un-reasonable punishment and little praise. Andry's findings are con-sistent with those of Bandura and Walters (1959) who reported that the relationship between delinquent sons and fathers is marked by rejection, hostility, and antagonism. Medinnus (1965) also obtained data suggesting a very high frequency of negative father-child rela-tionships among delinquent boys, and McCord, McCord, and Howard (1963) found that a deviant, aggressive father in the context of general parental neglect and punitiveness was strongly related to juvenile delinquency.

There is some evidence that boys who commit delinquent acts by themselves have more negative relationships with their fathers than do boys who commit delinquent acts with other gang members (Brigham, Ricketts, & Johnson, 1967). On the other hand, investi-gators have reported that boys who have positive relationships with their fathers are likely to engage in constructive and prosocial gang behavior (Crane, 1955; Thrasher, 1927). Such findings indicate that the quality of fathering a boy receives is of much influence in his peer relationships.

Interpersonal Relationships

Paternal deprivation can interfere with the development of successful peer relationships. Stolz et al.'s (1954) observations, as well as mothers' and fathers' reports, indicated that four- to eight-year-old children who had been father-absent for the first few years of life had poorer peer relationships than children who had not been father-absent. The Norwegian father-separated boys in Tiller's (1958) investigation were judged to have less adequate peer relationships than nonfather-separated boys. Other investigators have reported that continuously father-absent boys are less popular and have less satisfying peer relationships than do father-present boys (e.g., Leiderman, 1953; Miller, 1961; Mitchell & Wilson, 1967).

Paternally deprived boys are often handicapped in their peer relationships because they lack a secure masculine orientation. Sex-appropriate behavior is very important in the formation of friendships among elementary school children. For instance, Tuddenham (1951, 1952) found that the most popular boys in the first grade were those who were considered by their peers to be good sports, good at games, daring, not bashful, and "real boys." Gray (1957, 1959) reported similar results for fifth- to eighth-grade boys. In addition, boys who were rated high in popularity perceived themselves as more similar to their fathers than did boys who were rated low in popularity (Gray, 1959).

A positive father-son relationship gives the boy a basis for successful peer interactions. Rutherford and Mussen (1968) reported evidence indicating that nursery school boys who perceive their fathers as warm and nurturant are likely to be generous with other children. Fourth-grade boys in Leiderman's (1953; 1959) study who had high acceptance among their peers had warmer relationships with their fathers than did those with low peer acceptance. Cox's (1962) data also suggest a consistency between boys' relationships with their fathers and with their peers.

Payne and Mussen (1956) found that adolescent boys who were similar to their fathers in terms of responses to the California Personality Inventory were rated as more friendly by their teachers than were boys who had responses markedly different from their fathers. Mussen et al.'s (1963) study also revealed that positive father-son relationships were associated with successful peer interactions and self-confidence among adolescent males. Studying high school boys, Helper (1955) found that boys who perceived themselves as similar to their fathers were likely to be highly accepted by their peers. Lois

Hoffman's (1961) results indicated that boys from mother-dominant homes had much more difficulty in their peer relationships than did boys from father-dominant homes. Self-confidence, assertiveness, and overall competence in peer group interaction were related to a warm father-son relationship.

For boys, the presence of a masculine father, a positive father-son relationship, generally sex-appropriate behavior, and popularity with peers are strongly related. The absence of a warm affectionate relationship with an adult male, during which mutual enjoyment of sex-typed interests and activities takes place, can seriously interfere with the boy's social development. The case of the maternally overprotected boy is relatively easy to understand. His mother strongly discourages his participation in masculine peer group activities, and his interests are very different from his male contemporaries. The unmasculine boy seems particularly likely to search for platonic relationships with girls or to associate with unmasculine boys. The case of the paternally deprived boy who is well-motivated to be masculine seems more complex. During preadolescence and adolescence many father-absent boys feel that they have to continually prove themselves because they lack a secure masculine self-concept. However, lack of self-confidence and a high level of anxiety are not viewed as appropriate for males and can lead to further interpersonal difficulties.

A paternally deprived boy might have poor peer relationships despite rigid denial of anxiety and seeming bravado. The boy who continually challenges and/or berates others in his effort to prove his masculinity can become very unpopular, although he may be feared and respected by his peers. Father-absent boys can, of course, form close relationships with other children. In fact, masculine-striving father-absent boys are likely to form relationships with older boys. Such relationships often facilitate their personality development, but because of dependency on peer acceptance, paternally deprived boys may passively conform to the wishes of an older peer group. This is an expression of their desire to have the masculine role model they lack at home. A related factor in their seeking relationships with older males may be the threat to their insecure masculine images of not performing as well in athletic and physical competition as boys their own age.

Sexual behavior. The paternally deprived boy's search for a father-figure can often be involved in the development of homosexual relationships. West (1959) and O'Connor (1964) found that homosexual males, more often than neurotic males, had histories of long periods of father-absence during childhood. West (1967) reviewed much evidence which indicates that paternal deprivation is a frequent precursor in the development of homosexuality. Ineffectual fathering, together with an intense close-binding mother-child relationship is particularly likely to lead to the development of a homosexual pattern of behavior in males. A close-binding sexualized mother-son relationship seems more common in father-absent homes than in father-present homes and may, along with related factors, lessen the probability of the boy entering into meaningful heterosexual relationships. During childhood, a significant proportion of homosexuals have been discouraged by their mothers from participating in masculine activities and have often been rewarded for feminine behavior (e.g., Bieber, et al., 1962; Gundlach, 1969).

Adult sexual relationships are highly associated with earlier sex-role development. There is evidence which suggests that the male who develops a strong sense of masculinity in childhood is more successful in his adult heterosexual relationships (Kagan & Moss, 1962). Difficulty in forming lasting heterosexual relationships often appears to be linked to paternal deprivation. Andrews and Christensen's (1951) data suggested that college students whose parents had been divorced were likely to have frequent but unstable courtship relationships. Winch (1949; 1950) found that father-absence among college males was negatively related to degree of courtship behavior (defined as closeness to marriage). He also reported that a high level of emotional attachment to the mother was negatively related to degree of courtship behavior. In their interview study, Hilgard, Neuman, and Fisk (1960) detected that many men whose fathers died when they were children continued to be very dependent on their mothers, if their mothers did not remarry. For example, only one of the ten men whose mothers did not remarry seemed to manifest a fair degree of independence in his marital relationship.

Jacobson and Ryder (1969) did an exploratory interview study with young marrieds who suffered the death of a parent prior to marriage. Death of the husband's father prior to the age of 12 was associated with a high rate of marriage difficulty. Husbands, father-absent early in life, were described as immature and as lacking inter-personal competence. Participation in feminine-type domestic activities and low sexual activity were commonly reported for this group. In general, their marriages were relatively devoid of closeness and intimacy. In contrast, when the husbands had lost their fathers after the age of 12, they were more likely to be involved in positive marriage relationships.

Research by Pettigrew (1964) with lower-class blacks is consistent with the supposition that father-absent males frequently have difficulty in their heterosexual relationships. Compared to father-present males, father-absent males were "more likely to be single or divorced—another manifestation of their disturbed sexual identification" (p. 420). Pettigrew also cited evidence suggesting that black males are less masculine in certain facets of their sex-role behavior than are white males.

Because of frequent paternal deprivation, and maternal depreciation of maleness, lower-class black males often suffer in terms of their sex-role orientations, even though they may be quite masculine in other facets of their behavior. In two studies, both father-availability and sociocultural background were significantly related to what could be considered measures of sex-role orientation (Barclay and Cusumano, 1967; Biller, 1968b). Studying lower-class black and white lower-class boys, I did not find any clear-cut differences in sex-role preference or sex-role adoption. However, in terms of projective sex-role orientation responses (ITSC), black father-absent boys were the least masculine; there was no significant difference between white father-absent and black father-present boys; and white father-present boys were the most masculine.

A great deal of the heterosexual difficulty that many paternally deprived lower-class males experience is associated with their compulsive rejection of anything that they perceive as related to femininity. Proving that they are not homosexual and/or effeminate is a major preoccupation of many lower-class males. They frequently engage in a Don Juan pattern of behavior, making one conquest after another, and a stable emotional relationship with a female may not be formed even during marriage. The fear of again being dominated by a female, as they were as children, contributes to their need to continually exhibit their masculinity by new conquests. The perception of child rearing as an exclusively feminine endeavor also interferes with their interaction with children and helps perpetuate the depressing cycle of paternal deprivation in lower-class families. Although such a pattern of behavior seems particularly prevalent among lower-class black males, it is by no means exclusive to this group.

Personal Adjustment

Frequent opportunities for observing a competent adult male in a variety of problem-solving situations are important in the development of the boy's maturity and responsibility. Bronfenbrenner (1961) found that the amount of time adolescent boys spent with their fathers was positively related to the degree of leadership and responsibility that the boys displayed in school. On the basis of their findings, Mussen et al. (1963) concluded that instrumental achievement striving was more frequent among adolescent boys with adequate (affectionate) father-son relationships than among those with inadequate father-son relationships. Findings from some studies suggest that males who have been father-absent during childhood generally have lower achievement motivation and experience less career success than do males who have been father-present (McClelland, 1961; Terman & Oden, 1947; Veroff et al., 1960).

The father's interest and consistent participation contributes to the development of the child's self-confidence and self-esteem. In a study with elementary school boys, Coppersmith (1967) found that paternal involvement in limit-setting was associated with high self-esteem. In contrast, boys with low self-esteem were much more likely to be punished exclusively by their mothers. Rosenberg's (1965) results suggested a relationship between father availability and self esteem. Among adolescents, those who were father absent had lower self-esteem than those who were father-present, particularly when father absence had begun in early childhood.

The involved father can do much to help his child to function independently and competently, and to motivate him to achieve success. Rosen and D'Andrade (1959) observed that fathers of adolescent boys with high achievement strivings encouraged their sons' self-reliance and independence. The father's role in fostering independence and achievement often revolves around giving the boy a model and allowing him to make his own decisions. The quality of father-mother interactions is very important. The father who is dominated by his wife is not an effective model for his son. Many boys from maternally dominated families are dependent and unsuccessful in their academic performance (e.g., Devereux, Bronfenbrenner, & Suci, 1962; Elder, 1962; Smelser, 1963).

It is important that the father be involved in his family and be viewed as a salient family decisionmaker. The father who is decisive and competent and also allows his child to be independent facilitates his child's ability to cope with his environment. Paternal self-confidence, encouragement, and involvement can be important factors in the development of the boy's problem-solving skills and ability to think flexibly. However, paternal interference in the son's activities can hamper the boy's functioning (Busse, 1969; Rosen & D'Andrade, 1959). A domineering father as well as a domineering mother can undermine the boy's competency by not allowing him sufficient opportunity to solve his own problems. Paternal domination and rigid subordination of the mother and child by the father stifles the boy's achievement strivings (Strodtbeck, 1958).

Anxiety. Inadequate fathering is often associated with a high level of anxiety in children. The paternally deprived child's insecurity in his interpersonal relationships can contribute to feelings of anxiety and low self-esteem. In addition, the paternally deprived child may experience much anxiety because of an overly intense relationship with his mother (see Chapter 4). The father-absent child, in particular, is likely to encounter economic insecurity, and, depending on the reason for paternal absence, may be concerned with his father's well-being. Feelings of being different from other children may also increase his anxiety and perception of being inadequate.

A principal role of the father is to help the family deal with environmental problems, and the paternally deprived child may encounter more than his share of many seemingly unsolvable crises. Children with adequate and available fathers are exposed to a model who can realistically and creatively deal with some of the problems that a mother may not have the experience or time to solve.

In a study of nursery school children, Koch (1961) found that father-absent (eight boys and three girls) children exhibited more anxiety on a projective test than did a matched group from intact families. The father-absent children more often selected unhappy faces for the central child depicted in various situations. Stolz et al. (1954) reported that four- to eight-year-old children, father-absent the first few years of life while their fathers were away in military service, were more anxious than children whose fathers had been consistently present. Previously father-separated children were observed to be more anxious with peers and adults; in story completion sessions when the situation involved the father; and in terms of maternal reports of seriousness and number of fears. It is important to note that the fathers were not absent at the time of the study and were having stressful relationships with their children.

McCord, McCord, and Thurber (1962) analyzed social workers' observations of 10- to 15-year-old lower-class boys. They concluded that father-absent boys manifested more anxiety about sex than a matched group of father-present boys, although the difference concerning amount of general fearfulness was insignificant. In a retrospective study, Stephens (1961) asked social workers about their experiences with father-absent boys. Father-absent boys were described as being more effeminate and anxious about sex than were father-present boys. Leichty (1960) did not find any evidence that father-absence during early childhood was associated with castration anxiety in college males, although some of her findings did suggest that father-absence was related to anxiety concerning mother-father sexual interaction.

A high level of anxiety is often an outcome of inadequate sex-role development. Some investigators have found that males low in masculinity and/or those with inappropriate sex-role preferences are highly anxious (e.g., Mussen, 1961; Sutton-Smith & Rosenberg). Similarly, there is evidence which suggests that poor father-child relationships are related to both a high level of anxiety and poor sex-role adjustment (Beier & Ratzeburg, 1953; Lazowick, 1955). However, other research has revealed that highly masculine behavior is sometimes associated with intense anxiety (e.g., Gray, 1957; Webb, 1963).

It could, of course, be argued that there are many different types and/or definitions of anxiety and this may help to explain these seemingly contradictory findings. A *secure* sex-role development is accompanied by a relatively low degree of anxiety in most situations. Many boys who exhibit high masculine preferences and high masculine adoptions are actually quite insecure in their sex-role development. Sex-role anxiety may lead many paternally deprived boys to overcompensate and become hypermasculine in their behavior. Lack of a firmly masculine sex-role orientation can be reflected in overly rigid sex-role preference and sex-role adoption behavior. There may be a curvilinear relationship between anxiety and certain facets of masculine behavior, particularly in adolescence. For example, both boys very low and boys very high in masculinity of sex-role preference may be relatively anxious.

Chronic anxiety and poor adjustment seem uncommon among boys who have solid identifications with their fathers (Lynn, 1969; Schoeppe, Haggard & Havighurst, 1953). Evidence from a number of studies suggests that males who perceive themselves as being similar to their fathers, particularly when their fathers are masculine, are likely to be relatively free of serious psychological difficulties (Cava & Rausch, 1952; Heilbrun, 1962; Heilbrun & Fromme, 1965; Sopchak, 1952).

On the other hand, there are data which indicate a high incidence of adjustment problems for males who have experienced inadequate fathering. Cervantes' (1965) findings revealed an association between paternal inadequacy and the child's not completing high school. Studying Peace Corps volunteers, Suedfield (1967) discovered that those who were father-absent during childhood were much more likely not to complete their scheduled overseas tours than were those who had not been father-absent. Premature terminations were associated with problems of adjustment and conduct, and included some psychiatrically based decisions. There is other research which suggests that there is a relationship between father-absence in childhood and poor occupational adjustment and unemployment in adulthood (Gay & Tonge, 1967; Hall & Tonge, 1963).

Psychopathology

Research indicating a higher than average frequency of interpersonal and cognitive difficulties among paternally deprived individuals has already been reviewed. Thus, it is not surprising that many studies have suggested that father-absent children often act very immature and frequently have a high rate of behavior problems relating to school adjustment, both academic and interpersonal (e.g., Garbower, 1959; Gregory, 1965a; Hardy, 1937; Holman, 1953; Layman, 1960; Palmer, 1960; Risen, 1939; Rouman, 1956; Rowntree, 1955; Russell, 1957; Seplin, 1952; Tuckman & Regan, 1966; Wylie & Delgado, 1969).

An examination of the files of child guidance centers also reveals that both paternal deprivation and inadequate sex-role development are much more common among disturbed children than among children in the general population. However, methodological limitations make for problems in interpreting the findings of most studies linking father-absence with emotional disturbance in children. In particular, analyses in terms of sex of child and control groups of nonproblem children are not included.

There appears to be a high rate of father loss among patients hospitalized for attempting to commit suicide (e.g., Gay & Tonge, 1967; Robins, Schmidt, and O'Neal, 1957). Other evidence indicates that individuals who have been father-absent are more likely to exhibit, to a pathological degree, feelings of loss and depressed behavior (e.g., Beck, Sehti, & Tuthill, 1963; Haworth, 1964; Hill & Price, 1967; Keeler, 1954; Travis, 1933).

Beck, Sehti, and Tuthill (1963) found that paternal absence before the age of four was highly associated with depression, but other studies have suggested that loss of father between the ages of 10–14 is particularly predisposing to depression (Dennehy, 1966; Hill & Price, 1967). Loss of father due to death may be more strongly related to chronically depressed behavior than is loss of father due to other factors. Research concerning father-absence and depressed behavior, although of heuristic value, has not been carefully controlled. For instance, many of the subjects suffering from paternal loss have frequently also had a history of institutionalization.

Brill and Liston (1966) reported that loss of father due to death in childhood was not unusually high among mental patients. However, loss of father due to divorce or separation in childhood was much higher for individuals suffering from neurosis, psychosis, or personality disorders than for a number of different comparison groups. Rates of childhood father-absence are higher among adult patients classified as neurotic or schizophrenic than among the general population (e.g., Da Silva, 1963; Ingham, 1949; Madow & Hardy, 1947; Norton, 1952; Oltman, McGarry & Friedman, 1952; Wahl, 1954, 1956).

Gregory (1958; 1965b) critically evaluated many of the relevant studies and emphasized some of the methodological pitfalls in comparisons involving the relative incidence of mental illness among father-present and father-absent individuals. Lack of consideration of the possible effects of socioeconomic status is a major shortcoming of most of the studies. Cobliner (1963) reported some provocative findings which suggested that father-absence is more likely to be related to serious psychological disturbance in lower-class, as compared to middle-class, individuals. Middle-class families, particularly with respect to the mother-child relationship, may have more psychological as well as economic resources with which to cope with paternal deprivation.

Family functioning. Lack of paternal involvement and maternal domination of the family is particularly common in the development of psychopathology. There is a growing literature suggesting that father-present males having inadequate fathering, compared to those with adequate fathering, are much more likely to develop severe behavior disturbances (e.g., Alkire, 1969; Anderson, 1969; Eisenberg, 1957; Farina, 1960; Gerard & Siegal, 1950; Johnson & Meadow, 1966; Kayton & Biller, 1971; Lidz, Parker, & Cornelison, 1956; Piety, 1967; Warren & Cameron, 1950).

Some of the most intriguing and methodologically sound studies have provided observations of family functioning in standardized problem-solving situations. Mishler and Waxler (1968) and Schuham (1970) have found that high paternal involvement and decision-making are uncommon in families in which there is a severely disturbed son. In families with nondisturbed sons, the father is most often the ascendant figure, and mutually acceptable decisions are much more common (Schuham, 1970).

Adequate personality development is facilitated in families in which the father clearly represents the masculine role and the mother the feminine role. Kayton and I (1971) studied matched groups of normal, neurotic, paranoid schizophrenic, and nonparanoid schizophrenic adult males. We found that normal subjects perceived their parents as exhibiting sex-appropriate behaviors to a greater extent than did the disturbed subjects. A smaller proportion of individuals in the disturbed groups viewed their fathers as possessing masculine-instrumental traits, and particularly among the schizophrenic groups, their mothers as having feminine-expressive characteristics. Severely disturbed behavior is often associated with difficulties and/or abnormalities in sex-role development (e.g., Biller & Poey, 1969; Cheek, 1964; Gardner, 1967; Kayton & Biller, 1972; McClelland & Watt, 1968; Zeichner, 1955, 1956).

However, extremely severe psychopathology such as autism or childhood schizophrenia does not usually develop simply as a function of disturbed parent-child relationships. The child's genetic and/or constitutional predispositions often play an important part in determining the severity of his psychopathology as well as the quality of parent-child interactions. Most children are handicapped if they have experienced paternal deprivation or inadequacy. They may have much difficulty in their emotional and interpersonal development. But in the great majority of cases, insufficient or inappropriate fathering (and/or mothering) per se does not account for children who are unable to develop basic communication skills and to form interpersonal attachments. For example, the child's neurological malfunctioning or extreme tempermentally related hyper- or hypo-sensitivity can make it very difficult for the parent to respond in a positive manner. In some cases, constitutionally atypical children contribute to the development of psychopathology in their parents.

Summary

The father is a model for his child. His positive involvement facilitates the boy's cognitive functioning, his ability to control his impulses and to function independently and responsibly, and his overall interpersonal competence.

Much of the father's influence is related to his impact on the boy's sex-role development. Certain cognitive skills are relatively sex-typed, and mastery of the environment and problem solving is often learned in the context of masculine opportunities. When the boy has a warm relationship with a masculine and competent father, he is well on his way to learning how to master his social and physical environment. His ability to understand the world outside of his home, to plan for the future, and to cope with crises can all be facilitated by his experiences with his father.

Much of what the boy learns about the masculine role comes from peer group interactions. The boy who receives positive fathering is particularly well suited to both learn and effectively influence his peer group. He is motivated to interact with other males, but he is also independent enough to resist passive conformity. He is more likely to be a leader and is better able to communicate with his peers. He is more comfortable with his masculinity and has little need to prove himself by means of overcompensatory behavior.

Having observed his father's relationship with his mother, he has learned basic skills in interacting with females. He can communicate adequately with the opposite sex. He does not feel intimidated by women, yet he does not have to dominate them constantly. He can accept their femininity because he is secure in his masculinity. He can succeed in marriage as well as in his occupation. Because he has experienced positive fathering, he is also more able to be a successful father.

On the other hand, the paternally deprived boy is likely to have developmental difficulties. This is especially true if he comes from a generally disadvantaged background. Father-absence and/or father inadequacy can be particularly debilitating for the lower-class boy. He is more apt to experience difficulties in school, both academically and interpersonally. He may be threatened by the feminizing influence of the classroom and overgeneralize this attitude to many types of intellectual endeavors. He is likely to be insecure in his peer relationships as well as in his relationships with authority figures. Not having a consistently interested adult male with whom to interact, he may experience problems in learning to control his impulses. He may become tied to his mother, or may become equally as dependent on his peer group. He may be less able to act independently and competently. Lack of masculine behavior and/or a compensatory overstriving are more frequent among inadequately fathered boys than they are among adequately fathered boys.

Paternal deprivation has often been found to be associated with high anxiety and a proneness to the development of severe psycho-pathology. Inadequate fathering is a frequent concomitant of children's and adults' problems. More research is needed to determine why some paternally deprived children become emotionally disturbed and others do not. As stressed in Chapter 3, sociocultural variables and constitutional factors are very important in determining the impact of variations in fathering. The mother-child relationship is especially crucial in determining the influence that paternal deprivation may have on the developing child. In the next chapter the mother-child relationship is considered in much more detail.

5

The Mother-Son Relationship

This chapter contains a discussion of data concerning the mother's influence on the boy's personality development, with particular emphasis on the mother-son relationship in the paternally deprived family.

Mother's Evaluation of the Father

Maternal attitudes relating to the father can be an important factor in the sex-role and personality development of boys in intact homes. Pauline Sears (1953) noted that mothers of kindergarten boys who took the feminine role in doll play tended to be critical of their husbands. In a clinical study of academically underachieving boys, Grunebaum et al. (1962) observed that a contributing factor to the boys' difficulties was the mothers' perceptions that their husbands were inadequate and incompetent. Helper (1955) compared high school boys' self-descriptions with the boys' perceptions of their fathers. He found that son-father similarity was significantly related to the mother's approval of the father as a model for the child.

Bronfenbrenner (1958) pointed out that similarity of father and son ". . . does not necessarily mean that the child wanted to be like his father, that his motivation was *personally directed.*" He goes on to summarize Helper's findings as follows:

A boy is more likely to aspire to and take on characteristics that are typically masculine in our culture when his mother regards such characteristics as desirable; the fact that these characteristics are also possessed and approved by the father may be merely a reflection of the cultural norm and quite incidental to the child's learning process (p. 119).

Maternal attitudes are of critical significance when the boy is father-absent. In his study of children separated from their fathers during wartime, Bach (1946) described "curiously ambivalent aggressive-

83

affectionate father fantasies in some cases where maternal father-typing tended to be depreciative" (p. 76). Clinical cases dramatically illustrate how the mother's consistently derogatory comments about the absent father can contribute to the development of a negative self-concept and maladaptive behavior in his son (Diamond, 1957; Neubauer, 1960). As might be expected, maternal attitudes concerning the absent father influence the child's reaction when the father returns (Baxter, Horton, & Wiley, 1964; Stolz et al., 1954).

The mother's evaluation of the absent father can be much related to the reason for his being absent. Feelings of resentment and loneliness can be associated with many different reasons for husband absence, but it is usually easier for a mother to talk positively about a husband who has died than one who has deserted her (Benson, 1968). Discussing the absent father with her children may be very frustrating for the mother, and when the father is absent because of divorce or desertion, such discussion may be even more painful. It is very difficult to maintain a positive image of the father in the face of the conflict and competition concerning children that often takes place before, during, and after a divorce. Sociocultural factors can also influence the family's reaction to father absence. For example, divorce seems to be less acceptable and more disruptive for Catholic and Jewish families than for Protestant families (Rosenberg, 1965).

The father-child relationship prior to father absence and the child's age at the onset of the absence are very important factors in determining the extent of the influence of maternal attitudes toward the absent father. For example, the father-absent boy who has had a positive relationship with his father up until ten years of age is less likely to be influenced by negative maternal views concerning the father than the boy who was paternally deprived even before his father's absence. Unfortunately, there have not been systematic investigations of how the reason for father-absence at different developmental periods influences the mother-son relationship.

Matriarchal families. A striking example of the negative evaluation of the father occurs in matriarchal families. This type of family is very common in lower socioeconomic neighborhoods, and seems to be particularly prevalent among lower-class blacks (e.g., Pettigrew, 1964). There are black families of lower socioeconomic status in which the father is a respected and integral member, but there seem to be many more in which he is absent or a relatively peripheral member. Dai (1953) cogently described this phenomena:

One interesting feature of the broken home situation among Negroes is the dominance of the mother or mother substitutes, such as grandmothers, aunts, and sisters. This phenomenon may also be found in homes that are not broken, but in homes where the fathers are no longer important; they are, therefore, about as good as absent. Another related feature of the situation is the preference for girls shown by many Negro mothers and grandmothers (p. 558).

Dai's (1953) contention that girls are often preferred to boys by lower-class black women is consistent with Rohrer and Edmonson's (1960) findings. As part of their extensive research project, black women were interviewed concerning their adoption preferences. These women generally expressed preferences to adopt girls rather than boys. This clear-cut preference for girls by black females seems in marked contrast to the findings of a survey study at a large midwestern university by Dinitz, Dynes, and Clarke (1954). Their investigation revealed that a majority of females would prefer to have a male child as their first child; or if they could have only one child. The white middle class puts more value on the male role than on the female role (Brown, 1958; Lynn, 1959). However, this high valuation of maleness and masculinity is not supported by matriarchal black women. According to Rohrer and Edmonson (1960):

The matriarchs make no bones about their preference for little girls, and while they often manifest real affection for their boy children, they are clearly convinced that all little boys must inexorably and deplorably become men with all the pathologies of that sex (p. 161).

Sociocultural factors lessen the probability of long-term marriage relationships among lower-class blacks (Pettigrew, 1964). The instability of marriage relationships among lower-class blacks may be related to the fact that individuals with certain personality patterns are predisposed to become divorced and/or to seek out very tangential marriage relationships (Grønseth, 1957; Loeb & Price, 1966). Because of their inability to tolerate close relationships with men, some women marry men who, due to their personality functioning and/or occupational commitments, cannot get very much involved in family life. The wife's negative attitudes concerning men can be a central factor in the husband's decision to desert her and his children.

However, the mother who has a positive attitude concerning masculinity can facilitate her father-absent son's personality development. For instance, by praising the absent father's general competence in dealing with his environment and his strength and physical prowess, she may be able to help her son learn to value his own maleness. On the other hand, maternal depreciation of the father's masculinity can lead the young boy to avoid acting masculine at least until the time he comes into contact with his male peer culture.

Maternal attitudes concerning masculinity and men form a significant part of the mother-son relationship. The mother often views her husband and her son in a similar manner. Nevertheless, maternal reactions are not independent from individual differences in children. The degree to which a mother perceives her son as similar to his father is often related to the boy's behavioral and physical characteristics. For example, if the boy very much resembles his father, facially and physically, it is more likely that the mother will expect her son's behavior to approximate his father's than if there were little father-son resemblance.

Maternal Overprotection

Maternal overprotection is a frequent concomitant of paternal deprivation. In families in which maternal overprotection exists, the father generally plays a very submissive and ineffectual role (Levy, 1943). When fathers are actively involved with their families, they are usually very critical of having their children overprotected and they also serve as models for independent behavior. If the father is absent, the probability of a pattern of maternal overprotection is sometimes increased. The child's age at the onset of father-absence is an important variable. The boy who becomes father-absent during infancy or during his preschool years is more likely to be overprotected by his mother, but if father-absence begins when the boy is older, he may be expected to take over many of the responsibilities his father had previously assumed.

Stendler (1952) described two critical periods in the development of overdependency: (1) at around age nine months, when the child first begins to test out if his mother will meet his dependency needs; and (2) from two to three years of age, when the child must give up his perceived control of his mother and learn to act independently in culturally approved ways. Paternal deprivation during these periods can make the child prone to overdependency. Studying first grade children, Stendler (1954) observed that many of them who were rated as overdependent by their teachers came from families with high rates of father-absence. Among the 20 overdependent children, 13 lacked the consistent presence of the father in the home during the first three years of life, compared to only 6 of 20 in the control group. Moreover, the 6 relatively father-absent children in the control group had generally been without their fathers for a much shorter time than the overdependent children. The actively involved father discourages the mother's overprotecting tendencies and encourages independent activity, especially in the boy. Unfortunately, Stendler did not give separate data analyses for boys and girls.

Retrospective maternal reports compiled by Stolz et al. (1954) suggested that mothers whose husbands were away in military service tended to restrict their infants' locomotor activities to a greater extent than did mothers whose husbands were present. However, these findings might also be more meaningful if the researchers had presented separate analyses in terms of sex of child. Similar results were reported by Tiller (1958) in his study with mothers of eight- and nine-year-old Norwegian children. Compared to the control group mothers, those whose husbands were seldom home (sailor officers) were more overprotective, as judged by material interview data and by the children's responses to a structured doll play test. The Stolz et al. (1954) and Tiller (1958) investigations suggested that paternally deprived and maternally overprotected boys are particularly likely to suffer in terms of their masculine development. In her study of kindergarten boys. Pauline Sears (1953) reported that many boys who took the feminine role in doll play had mothers who restricted their sons' mobility outside the home. In a study of five-year-old children, I found that mothers of father-absent boys were less encouraging of independent and aggressive behavior than were mothers of father-present boys. Many of the informal responses of the husband-absent mothers indicated that they were particularly fearful of their children being physically injured (Biller, 1969b).

Physical status. The child's behavior and overall physical status can, of course, be a factor influencing maternal reactions. If a child is particularly frail, much maternal concern may be very realistic. Children who have had frequent or chronic illnesses are likely to have very close relationships with their mothers. In some cases constant maternal attention is necessary. Fathers often find it very difficult to interact with a chronically sick child, and relatively exclusive mother-child relationships often develop. Unfortunately, the intense mother-child relationship which was originally related to the child's illness frequently persists even after the child is well. For example, the mother may still perceive that her child needs to be protected from vigorous activities with other children. Such a situation can be very inhibiting to peer relationships and adequate sex-role development.

The mother whose child has been very sick in infancy may be prone to overreact to the child's later illnesses. She is apt to become overrestrictive and overprotective. The child, in turn, may receive much attention for reporting his complaints and physical discomforts. Males who have psychosomatic disorders have often had extremely close relationships with their mothers, poor relationships with their fathers, and inadequate sex-role development (e.g., Lipton, Steinschneider, & Richmond, 1966). There is also data which suggest that father-absent children are more likely than are father-present children to develop psychosomatic symptoms (e.g., Rosenberg, 1965). Of course, it is difficult to determine whether the familial situation was an etiological factor or merely an outcome of an originally circumscribed illness. There are physiologically based individual differences with respect to predispositions towards certain types of psychosomatic disorders (e.g., Lipton, Steinschneider, & Richmond, 1966). Whether family etiology is primary or secondary, maternal overprotection and paternal deprivation often lead to the development of maladaptive behavior patterns. Such familial factors also play a significant role in the development of alcoholism and drug addiction.

Sociocultural milieu. In assessing variables that influence the behavior of the husband-absent mother, economic and social difficulties cannot be overlooked (e.g., Glasser & Navarre, 1965; Hartley, 1960). Kriesberg (1967) poignantly described the plight of the mother whose husband is absent:

His absence is likely to mean that his former wife is poor, lives in poor neighborhoods, and lacks social, emotional, and physical assistance in childrearing. Furthermore, how husbandless mothers accommodate themselves to these circumstances can have important consequences for their children (p. 288).

The degree to which the husbandless mother has social and economic resources available to her can influence the child's interpersonal and educational opportunities. Taking such factors into consideration, the lower-class child seems even more disadvantaged by fatherlessness than does the middle-class child.

The mother's attitudes are related to her social and economic opportunities and are readily transmitted to the child. Maternal views concerning the worth of education are linked to sociocultural background. As a function of differing maternal values and reinforcement patterns, middle-class father-absent children are less handicapped in intellectual pursuits than are lower-class father-absent children. Middle-class father-absent boys appear to receive more maternal encouragement for school achievement than do lower-class father-absent boys (see also Chapter 4).

Sociocultural background is associated with the frequency of maternal overprotection. McCord, McCord, and Thurber (1962) found no evidence of maternal overprotection or overdependency among lower-class father-absent boys. Consistent with McCord, McCord, and Thurber's findings are the case studies of lower-class father-absent males presented by Kardiner and Ovesey (1951) and Rohrer and Edmonson (1960). A lower-class mother may have less opportunity to overprotect a father-absent child than does a middle-class mother, because she is more often engaged in a full-time job (Heckscher, 1967). There is less of a social stigma attached to father-absence by lower-class families, especially among lower-class black families (King, 1945). A mother without a husband who has young children is a more common phenomenon in the lower class. In contrast, the middle-class mother appears to be more predisposed to feel guilty if her child, particularly her son, is being deprived of a father. The middle-class mother seems more likely to overprotect and overindulge her child.

On the other hand, maternal rejection and neglect are quite common among husbandless lower-class mothers (e.g., Heckscher, 1967; McCord, McCord, & Thurber, 1962). Compared to middle-class mothers, lower-class mothers without husbands seem more concerned with their own needs and their day-to-day existence and often withdraw from their children. Lower-class mothers are particularly likely to reject their male children (Beller, 1967; Dai, 1953).

Either overprotection or rejection can reduce the probability of the boy's feeling a sense of worth in terms of his maleness. Maternal indifference or rejection makes a boy more prone to be indiscriminately influenced by the gang milieu than does maternal overprotection. The maternally overprotected paternally deprived boy may be quite timid and passive in peer interactions, whereas the maternally rejected father-absent boy is more likely to actively seek peer acceptance.

The frequent depreciation of maleness by their mothers contributes to the meaningfulness of the gang milieu for lower-class boys. A boy who is neglected or rejected can have his needs for attention, recognition, and affection satisfied by becoming a member of a gang. Masculine behaviors, particularly clear-cut acts of physical prowess and aggression, are highly valued by the gang, and behaviors perceived as feminine are anxiously avoided. The boy's physical status can also be a factor in determining whether he can achieve peer acceptance. The boy who is big and muscular will have a much greater chance of impressing his peers than the boy who is small and frail. If he has the ability to perform in an aggressive and competitive manner, participation in a gang milieu may help bolster the paternally deprived boy's self-image. However, the gang milieu often promotes rigid interpersonal and cognitive functioning. For example, many boys resent participation in intellectual endeavors, perceiving such activities as feminine.

Sex-role conflicts. Low paternal availability often leads to an increase in the intensity of the emotional relationship between mother and child, especially during infancy and early childhood. A strong and relatively exclusive attachment to his mother can severely hamper a boy's social and sex-role development. Barbara Miller (1961) discovered a negative relationship between degree of maternal attachment and masculinity of interests in lower-class adolescent boys. Winch's (1950) questionnaire data suggest that college males' courtship behavior is inversely related to their attachment to their mothers.

Anthropologists have described intense mother-child relationships which often develop in preliterate societies during postpartum taboos concerning sexual intercourse. Such taboos may last two to three years, during which time the family is relatively father-absent. In a cross-cultural investigation, Stephens (1962) presented evidence indicating that long postpartum taboos tend to make mothers closer to their children and less husband-centered. In societies with long postpartum taboos, mothers tend to be overprotective, as well as more indulgent of dependency than are mothers in societies in which postpartum taboos are of short duration. Cross-cultural data suggest that sex-role conflicts are frequent in societies in which young children have a relatively exclusive relationship with their mothers (e.g., Burton & Whiting, 1961; Stephens, 1962). Sociocultural variations, especially those reflected in terms of prevalent patterns of mothering, may account for marked differences between father-absent and father-present children in some societies but not in others (e.g., Ancona, Cesa-Bianchi, & Bocquet, 1964).

On the basis of his experience with middle class American families, Levy (1943) found that excessive physical contact was a frequent concomitant of maternal overprotection. Among 19 cases of maternal overprotection involving boys, 6 of the boys slept with their mothers long past infancy, 3 during adolescence. In almost one-half of Wylie and Delgado's (1959) cases involving father-absent preadolescent and adolescent boys, mother and son slept together in the same bed or bedroom. Sons often serve as husband-surrogates for husbandless mothers. In his review of psychoanalytic case studies, Neubauer (1960) emphasized how difficult sex-role development is for the young father-absent boy who has a highly sexualized relationship with his mother. Such an intense relationship affords the boy little opportunity to interact with masculine role models. In addition, the boy's inability to cope with his sexual feelings toward his mother may lead to a defensive feminine identification (Freud, 1947).

An intense relationship with the mother, and little opportunity to observe appropriate male-female interactions, is more common when the boy is paternally deprived. As discussed in Chapter 4, a close-binding mother-son relationship, in the context of paternal deprivation, is an important factor contributing to difficulties in heterosexual relationships and in the etiology of male homosexuality.

Stoller (1968) described the case histories of several boys who felt that they were really females. These boys represented an extreme in terms of the pervasiveness of their femininity. Stoller referred to them as being transsexual. These boys had extremely close physical relationships with their mothers. Mutual mother-child body contact during infancy was especially intense and there was much evidence that the mothers reinforced many forms of feminine behavior. In none of these cases was the father masculine or involved with his child. Stoller's book is replete with references to case studies suggesting that disturbed sex-role development in males is associated with an overly intense, relatively exclusive mother-son relationship.

In addition to lacking a male role model during the preschool years, the father-absent boy is likely to be confronted by a mother who does not encourage masculine behavior. As father-absent boys come into contact with boys from intact homes, especially as they begin school, they may be ignored or rejected because of their lack of masculine behavior. Many father-absent boys who are strongly motivated to adopt masculine behavior will do so if they have sufficient opportunity to interact with their peers. Their mothers may react negatively to such behavior—and thus create conflict, and some degree of sex-role confusion. The boy will learn to modify his behavior according to whether he is interacting with his mother or his peers, but the development of a secure sex-role orientation may be very difficult.

If a boy is extremely emotionally and instrumentally dependent upon his mother, he may not become involved in the masculine subculture. A boy with a strong but a less intense mother-son relationship can learn to act feminine in the presence of his mother and masculine with his peers. However, keeping behavior consistent with an internal standard of masculinity-femininity, which Kagan (1964) stressed as a central motivational process, can be very difficult and anxiety-producing for the father-absent boy.

The boy's sex-role conflicts are often manifested by difficulties in interacting with females. Ruth Hartley (1959) interviewed eight- to eleven-year-old boys from intact homes and delineated the following types of sex-role development: (1) overly intense masculine striving combined with rigidity concerning male and female activities and hostility toward women; (2) overly-intense masculine striving combined with rigidity concerning male and female activities but no hostility towards women; (3) inclinations and attempts to withdraw from the masculine role and related activities; and (4) a positively integrated and balanced sex-role. Behaviors related to (1), (2), and (3) are more frequently displayed by paternally deprived boys than by adequately fathered boys. However, in order to make meaningful predictions, peer group interactions, the quality of the mother-child relationship, and various family structure variables need to be carefully considered.

For example, birth order and age and sex of siblings can interact with maternal behavior to influence the father-absent child's personality development. If a father-absent boy is an only child or the only boy in an all female family, the probability of maternal overprotection is increased. On the other hand, if the boy has frequent opportunity to interact with older male siblings, peers, and adults, who encourage the development of his autonomy and assertiveness, the chance of a close-binding mother-son relationship is lessened.

The Mother's Sex-Role Development

A boy with a highly masculine mother is likely to have difficulties in his sex-role development. An important facet of the sex-role development process is learning how to interact with the opposite sex; and the boy with a masculine mother is at a disadvantage in trying to generalize his experiences to his relationships with other females. Masculine women often have sex-role conflicts. Such conflicts frequently are expressed in attempts to dominate males, including their sons. Case study data indicates that mothers with severe sex-role conflicts discourage their sons' masculine development (e.g., Bieber et al., 1962; Fenichel, 1945; Levy, 1943; Neubauer, 1960; Stoller, 1968).

Levy (1943) claimed that many of the maternally overprotecting mothers he studied had severe problems in sex-role identification. He speculated that their insecurity in being feminine was a factor in their inappropriate mothering techniques. Anxiety concerning their children's sexuality is common among mothers with sex-role conflicts. Sears, Rau, and Alpert (1965) found evidence suggesting that maternal sex anxiety was negatively associated with preschool-age boys' masculinity.

The boy's masculine development can be facilitated if his mother is secure in her femininity. Payne and Mussen (1956) found a negative correlation between mothers' and sons' scores on the Gough Femininity Scale; feminine scoring mothers tended to have masculine scoring sons. Steimel (1962) reported a tendency for boys with low masculine interests to perceive their mothers as having masculine interests. However, data from several other studies do not suggest that there is a clear-cut relationship between the sex-typing of mothers' and sons' interests (Angrilli, 1960; Mussen & Rutherford, 1963; Terman & Miles, 1936).

In terms of available data, the degree of femininity of the mother's interests does not appear to be critical, but the general role she assumes in her family does seem important. For example, a mother can express feminine interests and yet basically not feel very secure about being a woman and a mother. On the other hand, she can be involved in traditionally masculine-type activities and yet still interact with her children in a feminine-expressive manner.

Maternal employment. Many mothers are employed and have demanding extrafamilial responsibilities. In a post-hoc analysis of data from her study of lower-class adolescents, Barbara Miller (1960) found that maternal employment was negatively related to masculinity of interests among father-present boys, but positively related to masculinity of interests among father-absent boys. She speculated that maternal employment in the lower-class father-present family may imply that the father is inadequate, whereas in the father-absent family the mother who works may present her son with a model of competence and independence. Nye (1959) reported a tendency for father-absent children whose mothers were employed to be better adjusted than those whose mothers were not employed. Such findings are interesting, but there seems to be a lack of other research dealing with the possible differential effects of maternal employment on father-absent and father-present children.

Maternal employment does seem to have an impact on the child's perception of the male and female role. Hartley and Klein (1959) investigated the relationship between maternal employment and the sex-role perceptions of elementary school children. Children who had working mothers made fewer sex-appropriate distinctions on a sorting task involving sex-typed occupations than did children who had nonworking mothers. Studying college students, Vogel et al. (1970) found that those with working mothers had less polarized views of sex differences than did those with nonworking mothers. However, the groups did not differ in terms of the masculinity-femininity of their self-perceptions.

The mother's having a more prestigious job than the father can be a disruptive factor in the child's sex-role development. In such a situation, it is more likely that the family will be maternally dominated. There does not appear to be any systematic research concerning how such factors might influence the boy's masculine development, but more marital conflicts are reported in families in which the wife has a better job than the husband (Gover, 1963; Roth & Peck, 1951).

Maternal employment per se does not seem to have a clear-cut effect on the child's personality development (Yarrow, 1964). What seems to be important is how the mother feels about being a woman and how secure she is in her basic femininity. The quality of mothering and fathering a child receives is of much more significance than whether or not his mother is employed. The next section includes evidence and speculation relating to the facilitating effects that particular types of mothering can have on the boy's personality development.

Effective Mothering

The mother-son relationship can stimulate or hinder adequate personality development. When the boy is paternally deprived, his relationship with his mother is particularly influential. McCord, McCord, and Thurber (1962) analyzed social workers' observations of 10- to 15-year-old lower-class boys. The presence of a rejecting and/or disturbed mother was related to various behavior problems (sexual anxiety, regressive behavior, and criminal acts) in father-absent boys, but father-absent boys who had seemingly well-adjusted mothers were much less likely to have such problems.

Pedersen (1966) compared a group of emotionally disturbed boys with a group of nondisturbed boys. The boys were all from military families and ranged in age from 11 to 15. Relatively long periods of father-absence were common for both the emotionally disturbed and nondisturbed children. However, it was only in the disturbed group that degree of father-absence was related to level of emotional disturbance (measured by the Rogers Test of Personality Adjustment). Pedersen also found that the mothers of the emotionally disturbed children were themselves more disturbed (in terms of MMPI responses) than were the mothers of the nondisturbed children. An implication of these findings is that psychologically healthy mothers may be able to counteract some of the effects of paternal deprivation.

Using a retrospective interview technique, Hilgard, Neuman, and Fisk (1960) studied adults whose fathers had died when they were children. These investigators concluded that the mother's ego strength was an important determinant of her child's adjustment as an adult. Mothers who could utilize their own and outside resources, and assume some of the dual functions of mother and father with little conflict, appeared to be able to constructively deal with the problems of raising a fatherless family. Such women were described as relatively feminine while their husbands were alive but as secure enough in their basic sex-role identifications to perform some of the traditional functions of the father after he had died. It is important to emphasize that the mother's ego strength rather than her warmth or tenderness seemed to be the essential variable in her child's adjustment. If a child is paternally deprived, excessive maternal warmth and affection may be particularly detrimental to his personality development. A close-binding overprotective relationship can severely hamper his opportunities for interpersonal growth.

When a mother is generally competent in interpersonal and environmental interaction, she may be an important model for her child.

However, a child's personality development seems to be facilitated only if the parent allows him sufficient freedom and responsibility to imitate effective parental behaviors (Biller, 1969a). For example, the young boy from a typical matriarchal family is often not encouraged to display assertive behavior. Matriarchal mothers often interfere with their son's attempts at mastery, and reward submissive responses. Such women seem to be insecure in terms of their underlying femininity and have difficulty in their interactions with males.

Maternal encouragement. Colley (1959) suggested that "even in a father's absence, an appropriately identified mother will respond to the boy 'as if' he were a male and will expect him to treat her as a male would treat a female" (p. 173). In intact homes, fathers seem to vary their own behavior more as a function of sex of child than do mothers. Fathers are reported to be more concerned with sex-typing and to more often base their expectations and reinforcements on the basis of sex of child (e.g., Goodenough, 1957; Tasch, 1955). In the paternally deprived home, the degree to which the mother can take over the sex-role differentiation function is of critical importance in the child's personality development.

A mother can facilitate her father-absent son's sex-role development by having a positive attitude toward the absent father and males in general, and by consistently encouraging masculine behavior in her son. In intact homes, parental reactions to aggressive and assertive behavior do influence the boy's personality development. For example, in Sears, Alpert, and Rau's (1965) investigation with nursery school children, parents who permitted and accepted aggressive and assertive behavior in their preschool-age sons had highly masculine sons. In contrast, boys low in masculinity were found to have parents who were anxious, nonpermissive, and severely punishing of aggression. In the context of warm parent-child relationships, restrictive and autocratic parents tend to have passive, conforming, and dependent children, whereas permissive and democratic parents tend to have active, assertive, and independent children (e.g., Baldwin, Kalhorn, & Breese, 1949; Becker, 1964).

Maternal encouragement of masculine behavior seems particularly important for the father-absent boy. In a study of kindergarten boys, I assessed maternal encouragement of masculine behavior with a multiple choice questionnaire (Biller, 1969b). The measure of maternal encouragement of masculine behavior was significantly related to the father-absent boy's masculinity, as assessed by a game preference measure and a multidimensional rating scale filled out by teachers. Father-absent boys whose mothers accepted and reinforced assertive, aggressive, and independent behavior were more masculine than father-absent boys whose mothers discouraged such behavior. Degree of maternal encouragement for masculine behavior was not significantly related to the father-present boys' masculine development.

The father-son relationship appears to be more critical than the mother-son relationship when the father is present, and it can be predicted that maternal encouragement and expectations concerning sex-role behavior are less important when the father is present than when he is absent. For instance, a warm relationship with a masculine and salient father can outweigh the effects of a mildly overprotective mother. However, maternal behavior is an especially significant variable in facilitating, or inhibiting, masculine development in the young father-absent boy. The mother can, by reinforcing specific responses and expecting masculine behavior, increase the father-absent boy's perception of the incentive value of the masculine role. Such maternal behavior can, in turn, promote a positive view of males as salient and powerful—and thus motivate the boy to imitate their behavior.

Father-absence generally has more of a retarding impact on the boy's sex-role orientation than it does on his sex-role preference or his sex-role adoption (see Chapter 1). Sex-role preference and sex-role adoption seem more easily influenced by maternal behavior. However, if a father-absent boy develops a masculine preference and adoption on the basis of both consistent maternal and peer group reinforcement, he is likely to view himself and his masculinity positively, and to develop a masculine sex-role orientation at least by his middle school years.

Father-absence before the age of five appears to have more effect on the boy's masculine development than does father-absence after the age of five, and it may be that the mother-child relationship is particularly crucial when the boy becomes father-absent early in his life. Bahm and I found that degree of perceived maternal encouragement for masculine behavior was highly related to the masculinity of junior high school boys who had been father-absent since before the age of five. (Perceived maternal encouragement for aggressive behavior was assessed by the subjects' responses to a Q-sort procedure, and their masculinity by their self-descriptions on an adjective check list.) Among the boys who became father-absent before the age of five, those who perceived their mothers as encouraging assertive and aggressive behavior had much more masculine self-concepts than did those who perceived their mothers as discouraging such behavior (Biller & Bahm, 1971).

Future research should lead to a much clearer delineation of the kinds of maternal behaviors, and the dimensions of the mother-child relationship, that are relevant to the father-absent boy's personality development. In Chapter 6, some research concerning the effects of father-absence on the girl's personality development is reviewed, and it is important for investigators studying the impact of father-absence to systematically examine the possible differential effects of the mother-child relationship as a function of sex of child. Data from such studies can be useful for programs designed to maximize the interpersonal and intellectual potential of father-absent children, and to help mothers in father-absent families to become more effective parents.

Summary

The mother's evaluation of the father can be an important determinant in the boy's personality development. If the mother is constantly critical of the father, it can interfere with the boy's viewing himself positively. When a boy is father-absent, the mother's view of the father may have particularly strong consequences. Mothers who feel abandoned or deserted by their husbands often develop a negative attitude toward males. Mothers in matriarchal homes devalue their sons and the masculine role.

In matriarchal families and in families in which there is maternal overprotection, there is generally paternal deprivation. If the father is present, he plays a submissive and ineffectual role. When fathers are absent or uninvolved, the probability of maternal domination and/or maternal overprotection is much increased. Mothers who excessively restrict their sons and consistently reward dependent behavior are likely to interfere with their son's psychological development. Maternal overprotection inhibits the development of independent and responsible behavior. Paternal deprivation also is often associated with a highly intense close-binding mother-child relationship. The boy's excessive emotional dependency on his mother can hamper his peer relationships and his heterosexual development.

Lower-class boys seem less likely to be maternally overprotected than do middle-class boys. However, the incidence of matriarchal homes is greater among the lower-class. In addition, the lower-class paternally deprived boy more often seems to rebel against his unmasculine family environment and to engage in overcompensatory gang behavior. The lower-class boy is more often maternally neglected or rejected than the middle-class boy. He seems to be more influenced by his peers and often develops a very negative attitude toward any endeavors that he perceives as feminine.

Although the probability of an inappropriate mother-son relationship is increased when the father is absent, it is clear that the mother can positively influence her paternally deprived son's personality development. Mothers who are psychologically healthy and competent can be models for effective behavior. The mother's security in her femininity is very important. If she feels comfortable in interacting with males and in accepting and encouraging a male's masculine responses, she can do much to aid in her son's masculine development.

When the father is absent or ineffectual, the mother-child relationship appears to assume more importance. In the father-present home, a warm relationship with a masculine father can outweigh the effects of an overprotecting mother, but in the father-absent home an overprotective mother can greatly interfere with her son's personality development. On the other hand, if a boy has a passive and ineffectual father who is frequently available to imitate, the mother might find it difficult to foster her son's masculine development. The mother of the father-absent boy may have more of an opportunity to encourage the boy's masculine development than the mother of the boy who has an available but inadequate father. The former does not have to counteract the influence of an inadequate model.

The effects of the mother-child relationship cannot be fully understood if they are considered in isolation from the father-child relationship, and the child's constitutional characteristics, sociocultural background, and peer relationships. For example, if the child is father-absent, the length and age of onset of father-absence should be taken into account; when boys become father-absent early in life, the mother-child relationship may be especially influential.

Fathering and Female Personality Development

The father's impact upon personality development has been increasingly recognized by contemporary theorists and researchers. However, the emphasis has been on the father-son relationship with relatively little acknowledgment being given to the importance of the father-daughter relationship. In the present chapter, an attempt is made to review ideas and findings which relate to the influence of fathering on the personality development of the female.

Feminine Development

Much of the influence of the father-daughter relationship is related to the girl's feminine development (e.g., Biller & Weiss; Johnson, 1963). Before examining hypotheses and research concerning the father-daughter relationship, it is important to analyze the meaning of femininity. Feminine development can be defined as the process by which a girl learns a complex pattern of behaviors which are consistent with the role expectations of her society. Much perceptual and cognitive learning is involved in feminine development (e.g., Hartley, 1964; Kohlberg & Zigler, 1966). The girl generally develops a feminine self-concept early in life, and her sex-role preference and overt behavior are usually related to her basic sex-role orientation.

Some observers have noted that there has been a marked tendency to define femininity in negative terms and/or as the opposite of masculinity; for instance, stressing passivity and dependency (e.g., Bieliauskas, 1965; Salzman, 1967). Using a group of college students as judges, Rosenkrantz et al. (1968) assessed cultural stereotypes of masculinity and femininity. An inspection of the 41 items on which there was 75 percent or better agreement, yielded a relatively negative definition of femininity. Although some items reflected positive feminine qualities, many items related to passivity, dependency, narcissism, and irresponsibility. Femininity, as traditionally defined, appears to involve passivity, dependency, an internal focus on a world

103

of emotion and fantasy rather than an inclination towards thought and action. Data from the Rosenkrantz et al. study indicate that college students view the feminine role as much less socially desirable than the masculine role.

Value judgments are made, to some extent, in definitions of appropriate sex-role behavior. Obviously, one has to base any definition of sex-roles in relation to a particular sociocultural milieu. Since a focus of the present discussion is on ways in which the father can facilitate his daughter's personality development, it is relevant to analyze elements of femininity which are related to psychological adjustment. It is meaningful to define feminine behavior in positive terms. For example, femininity in social interaction is related to skill in interpersonal communication, expressiveness of warmth, and sensitivity to the needs of others. There is empirical support for this point of view. Studying preschool-age children, Vroegh et al. (1967) found that a high degree of femininity in young girls was related to social adjustment, competence, and self-confidence. Other research has also suggested an association between feminine behavior, interpersonal adjustment, and confidence in women (e.g., Douvan & Adelson, 1966; Pinter & Fortano, 1944; White, 1959).

Parsons (1955) has differentiated masculinity and femininity on the basis of the predominance of instrumental needs, interests and functions in the former and of *expressive* needs, interests, and functions in the latter. Men are seen as assuming more technical, executive, and judicial roles; women more supportive, integrative, and tension-managing roles. In a study emanating from the Parsonian framework, Heilbrun (1965b) obtained ratings from four clinical psychologists as to the instrumental or expressive nature of the adjectives included in Gough & Heilbrun's Adjective Check List. Femininity, as reflected in the expressive adjectives, consists of warmth, sensitivity to the needs of others, the ability to communicate positive feelings, and general social competence.

The girl's perception of herself, and of the value of feminine behavior, can be much influenced by family structure. For example, girls with sisters tend to be more feminine than girls with brothers (e.g., Brim, 1958). The family's sociocultural background also can be very influential. Girls in upper-middle-class homes appear to be much less satisfied with the traditional feminine role than do lower-middle-class girls (e.g., Hartley, 1964). The domestic role is often devalued in homes in which there is emphasis on professional accomplishment and the opportunity for the mother to turn over certain household responsibilities to a person of lower status. However, it is important to point out that femininity, according to the present definition, is based upon a positive feeling about being a female—and a particular patterning of interpersonal behavior. Whether or not a woman enjoys housework, or chooses a career, should not be used as the ultimate criterion in assessing her femininity.

The child is not merely a passive recipient of familial and socio-cultural influences. As has been stressed in earlier sections of this book, the child's constitutional predispositions can play a very important part in influencing parent-child and environmental inter-actions. For example, the young girl who is tempermentally re-sponsive to social interaction and is very attractive may make it especially easy for her father to encourage her feminine development. Similarly, if the girl facially and physically resembles a highly feminine mother, the father is likely to treat her as a female. On the other hand, the girl who is physically large and unattractive may be per-ceived as unfeminine by her father. The father is more likely to reject his daughter if she does not fit his conception of the physical charac-teristics of femininity. If the father does not have a son and his daughter is particularly vigorous and well coordinated, he may treat her as if she were a boy.

Fathering and Femininity

A basic phase of the girl's sex-role development involves the positive acceptance of herself as a female. The father-daughter relationship is particularly important. The father can foster the establishment of a positive feminine sex-role orientation by treating his daughter as a female and encouraging her to value her femininity.

The traditional psychoanalytic view of feminine development gave some recognition to the importance of father's role (e.g., Freud, 1924, 1935). Emphasis was placed upon the girl's oedipal relation-ship with her father. It was speculated that during the oedipal period the little girl detached herself from her mother and began to develop an erotic attitude toward the father. The passivity of the girl in her relationship with her father was stressed. According to Deutsch (1944), the father showers his daughter with affection and tenderness when she acts passive, helpless, and/or femininely seductive, but discourages her masculine and/or aggressive strivings. Many psycho-analytic theorists tend to view femininity in a rather negative context (e.g., they emphasize passivity, dependency, and a masochistic attitude).

Leonard (1966) also discussed the father-daughter relationship in a psychoanalytic framework but seemed to take a somewhat more positive view of femininity. Leonard contended that the girl must establish an affectionate relationship with her father in order to later be able to form a love relationship with a male her own age. If the girl is paternally deprived or father-absent, she may idealize her father and later, as an adolescent, seek a love object similar to this ideal, never being satisfied with the men she meets. Alternatively, she may maintain a very immature narcissistic attitude, so that she has the extreme need to receive love but lacks the capacity to give love. Leonard speculated that a father who rejects or ignores his daughter may contribute to her remaining at a phallic, masculine-identified phase of development. In this situation the daughter hopes to receive the love of both parents: the mother's love because the daughter is similar to the father whom the mother loves; and the father's love because the daughter has become the boy he once was, or the son he wished for.

Such learning theorists as Mowrer (1950) and Sears (1957) focused upon the importance of parental nurturance in the rewarding of the child's sex-appropriate behaviors. They hypothesized that the child becomes strongly dependent on the parents for supplying nurturance and learns to perform those behaviors which the parents reward. Learning theorists do not generally attach special significance to the father-daughter relationship. However, in terms of the father's ability to reward particular behaviors it can be argued that he has a signifi-cant influence on his daughter's personality development. Paternal reinforcement of the girl's attempts to emulate her mother's behavior, and the father's general approval of the mother's behavior, seem particularly important.

Parsons (1955; 1958) emphasized the role of the father in feminine development more than have psychoanalytic and learning theorists. He viewed the mother as very influential in the child's general personality development—but not as significant as the father in the child's sex-role functioning. He emphasized that the mother does not vary her role as a function of the sex of the child as much as does the father. According to Johnson, the mother has a primarily expressive relationship with both boys and girls; in contrast, the father rewards his male and female children differently, encouraging instrumental behavior in his son and expressive behavior in his daughter. The father is supposed to be the principal transmitter of culturally based conceptions of masculinity and femininity (Johnson, 1963).

Paternal differentiation. The girl's feminine development is much influenced by how the father differentiates his masculine role from her feminine role. Studying first grade children, Mussen and Rutherford (1963) found that fathers of highly feminine girls encouraged their daughters more in sex-appropriate activities than did fathers of unfeminine girls. These investigators suggested that masculine fathers who actively encourage and appreciate femininity in girls are particularly able to facilitate their daughter's sex-role development. Similarly, in their study with nursery school children, Sears, Rau, and Alpert (1965) reported a significant correlation between girls' femininity and their fathers' expectations of their participation in feminine activities.

In an examination of the familial antecedents of sex-role behavior, Heilbrun (1965b) concluded that fathers are more proficient in differentiating between their male and female children. Heilbrun emphasized that "fathers are more capable of responding expressively than mothers are of acting instrumentally . . . that fathers systematically vary their sex-role as they relate to male and female offspring" (p. 796). The more a father participates in constructive interplay with his daughter, and the more this interaction involves the opportunity for her to learn specific behaviors defining her feminine role, the more adequate will be her sex-role development.

Tasch (1952; 1955) interviewed fathers of boys and girls in order to learn their conceptions of the paternal role. She found much evidence of paternal differentiation in terms of sex of child. Her results indicated that fathers viewed their daughters as more delicate and sensitive than their sons. Fathers were found to use physical punishment more frequently with their sons than with their daughters. Fathers tended to define household tasks in terms of their sex-appropriateness. For example, they expected girls to iron and wash clothes and babysit for siblings, while boys were expected to be responsible for taking out the garbage and helping their fathers in activities involving mechanical and physical competence.

Goodenough's (1957) results support the view that fathers influence their children's sex-role development more than do mothers. She focused upon the influence of the parents in determining the social interests of nursery school children. She found that "... the father has a greater interest in sex differences than the mother and hence exerts stronger influence in general sex-typing" (p. 321). For example, there was much more paternal encouragement for girls to develop skills in social interaction. Much paternal emphasis on sex-role differentiation was also found in a study by Aberle and Naegele (1952). Differences in parent-child interactions are a function of sex of child as well as sex of parent (e.g., Bronfenbrenner, 1961; Papenek, 1969; Rosenberg & Sutton-Smith, 1968; Rothbart & Maccoby, 1966).

Paternal involvement. When the father is not involved in the family, his daughter is likely to have sex-role development problems. Lois Hoffman (1961) found that girls from mother-dominant homes had difficulty relating to the opposite sex and were disliked by boys. However, Hetherington (1965) did not find a relationship between parental dominance and girls' sex-role preferences. Other studies are also consistent with the supposition that paternal dominance is a less crucial factor for girls than it is for boys (Biller, 1969c; Hetherington & Frankie, 1967).

My (1969c) results suggested that the girl's feminine development is facilitated if the mother is seen as a generally salient controller of resources. In this study, kindergarten-age girls perceived their fathers as more competent and decisionmaking, their mothers as more limit-setting, and both parents as similar in nurturance. There was a subgroup of girls whose femininity scores were low and who perceived their mothers as relatively high in decisionmaking and limit-setting, but quite low in nurturance and competence. In most cases, at least a moderate level of paternal involvement in decision-making seemed important in the girl's feminine development.

For girls the *optimal level* of paternal dominance may be moderate, allowing the mother to also be viewed as a salient controller of resources. It is important that the girl perceive her father as masculine and as warmly appreciating her feminine behavior, even if she does not perceive him as the dominant parent. Findings from several investigations have pointed to the influence of positive paternal involvement in the girl's interpersonal development (Baumrind & Black, 1967; Fish & Biller, 1970; Torgoff & Dreyer, 1961).

The results of an investigation by Fish and me (1972) also suggest that the father plays an important role in the girl's personality adjustment. College girls' perceptions of their relationships with their fathers during childhood were assessed by means of an extensive family background questionnaire. Subjects who perceived their fathers as having been very nurturant, and positively interested in them, scored high on the Adjective Check List personal adjustment scale. In contrast, subjects who perceived their fathers as having been rejecting scored very low on the personal adjustment measure.

Other data reveal long-term consequences of the father-daughter relationship. In Winch's (1950; 1951) questionnaire study, with college students, females who had long-term romantic relationships (who appeared near marriage) reported closer relationships with their fathers than did females who did not have serious heterosexual involvements. Luckey (1960) found that women who were satisfied with their marriages perceived their husbands as more similar to their fathers than did women who were not satisfied in their marriages. The female's ability to have a successful marriage relationship is increased when she has experienced a warm affectionate relationship with a father who has encouraged her feminine development.

Women often choose to pursue a full-time career rather than marriage because of very realistic factors, such as self-fulfillment and economic need. However, the choice of a career can be motivated by a fearful avoidance of marriage. Unmarried career women frequently have much underlying sex-role conflict (Levin, 1966). In Rushing's (1964) study with adolescents, girls who had satisfactory relationships with their fathers were less likely to aspire to careers than were those who had unsatisfactory relationships with their fathers. When a girl is continually frustrated in her interactions with her father, she may develop a negative attitude toward close relationships with men and marriage. White (1959) compared the self-concepts and familial backgrounds of women whose interests focused on marriage and child rearing with those whose interests revolved around a career. More of the women who were interested in marriage appeared to have close relationships with both parents and to be comfortable in their self-concepts. More of the women interested in careers came from homes in which the father had died or in which there was inadequate parent-child communication.

Father Absence

As is emphasized in previous chapters, the specific effects of paternal absence are influenced by such factors as the personality of the mother, sociocultural background, and the presence and sex of siblings. However, it can be expected that with such factors held constant, the consequences of paternal absence include certain disadvantages for the girl as well as the boy. For example, the father-absent girl may lack certain experiences which make it difficult for her to interact with males.

Father-absence can interfere with the girl's feminine development and her overall heterosexual adjustment. In Seward's (1945) study, women who rejected the feminine role of wife and mother were more likely to come from broken homes than were women who accepted these roles. White (1959) reported similar results. Landy, Rosenberg, and Sutton-Smith (1967) found that, among college females, father-absence during adolescence was associated with low femininity of interests. Although she studied father-present females, Fish's (1969) data also seem relevant. Females who reported a lack of father availability in childhood had less feminine self-concepts than did those who reported moderate or high father availability.

In Jacobson and Ryder's (1969) interview study, many women who had been father-absent early in life complained of difficulties in achieving satisfactory sexual relationships with their husbands. Lack of opportunity to observe meaningful male-female relationships in childhood can make it much more difficult for the father-absent female to develop the interpersonal skills necessary for adequate heterosexual adjustment. Case studies of father-absent girls are often filled with details of problems concerning interactions with males, particularly in sexual relationships (e.g., Leonard, 1966; Neubauer, 1960).

There is evidence that father-absent girls are overly dependent on their mothers. Lynn and Sawrey (1959) examined the effects of frequent father-absence upon eight to nine and one-half-year-old boys and girls. They compared children whose fathers were sailors—absent at least nine months a year—with a matched group of children who had not been separated from their fathers (see Chapter 1 for further discussion of this study). Structured doll play data indicated that the father-separated girls manifested greater than average dependency upon their mothers. Helper's (1955) findings suggest that a high degree of dependency on the mother is associated with low peer status for high-school girls.

Some research indicates that the father-absent girl often has difficulty in dealing with her aggressive impulses. In their doll play study, Sears, Pintler, and Sears (1946) found "no indication that the girls are more frustrated when the father is present; on the contrary, his absence is associated with greater aggression, especially self-aggression" (p. 240). These investigators speculated that a high degree of aggressive doll play behavior may be a function of the father-absent girl's conflict with her mother. Heckel (1963) observed frequent school maladjustment, excessive sexual interest, and social acting-out behavior in five fatherless preadolescent girls. Other investigators have also found a high incidence of delinquent behavior among father-absent girls (Monahan, 1957; Toby, 1957). Such acting-out behavior may be a manifestation of frustration associated with the girl's unsuccessful attempts to find a meaningful relationship with an adult male.

Father-absence seems to increase the probability that a girl will experience difficulties in interpersonal adjustment. Many studies referred to in Chapter 4 suggested that father-absent girls are likely to have emotional and social problems. But one difficulty in interpreting many of these studies is that they do not differentiate boys and girls in data analyses.

The devaluation of maleness and masculinity, so prevalent in paternally deprived matriarchal families, adversely affects many girls as well as boys. Children in lower-class families often do not have opportunities to interact with adequate fathers. In lower-class families father-daughter relationships are generally not very adequate. The father may be very punitive and express little affection towards his daughter (Elder & Bowerman, 1963). Many investigators have observed that black girls, in families in which the father is absent or ineffectual, develop derogatory attitudes toward males (e.g., Pettigrew, 1964). In a study with disadvantaged black children, Santrock (1970a) found a tendency for father-absent girls to be more feminine on a doll play sex-role measure than were father-present girls; a very high level of femininity may be associated with a rigid sex-role development which devalues masculine activities.

The downgrading of males in terms of their seeming social and economic irresponsibility is common among lower-class black families. Negative attitudes towards males are transmitted by mothers, grandmothers, and other significant females, and unfortunately, are often strengthened by the child's observation or involvement in destructive male-female relationships. Paternal deprivation, in the rubric of the devaluation of the male role, is a major factor in the lower-class females' frequent difficulties in interacting with their male relatives, boyfriends, husbands, and children. Maternally based households seem to become like family heirlooms—passed from generation to generation (Rohrer & Edmonson, 1960).

Inadequate Fathering

The father-mother interaction can have much impact on the child's personality development. Family stability and cohesiveness helps to provide a positive atmosphere for the developing child. An inadequate father is often also an inadequate husband. The father may influence his daughter's personality development indirectly in terms of his relationship with his wife. If the father meets his wife's needs she may, in turn, be able to interact more adequately with her children. Bartemeier (1953) emphasized that the wife's capacity for appropriately nurturing her children, and her general psychological adjustment, is much influenced by her relationship with her husband. A number of investigations have indicated that a warm and nurturant mother-daughter relationship is important in feminine development (e.g., Hetherington, 1965; Hetherington & Frankie, 1967; Mussen & Parker, 1965; Mussen & Rutherford, 1963).

Inadequate fathering or mothering may be a reflection of difficulties in the husband-wife relationship. Such difficulties may be particularly apparent in the husband's and wife's inability to adequately provide one another with affection and sexual satisfaction. The parents' interpersonal problems are usually reflected in their interactions with their children and in their children's adjustment. For example, clinical studies have revealed that difficulties in parental sexual adjustment, combined with overrestrictive parental attitudes, are often associated with incestuous and acting out behavior among adolescent females (e.g., Kaufman, Peck & Tagiuri, 1954; Robey et al., 1964).

Severe marital conflict can have a disorganizing effect on both paternal and maternal behavior. Baruch and Wilcox's (1944) results indicated that marital conflict negatively influences the personality development of both boys and girls. Some of their data suggested that girls can be even more handicapped than boys. Girls may suffer more because of their interpersonal sensitivity. On the basis of some research findings, familial factors seem to have more impact on girls' than on boys' personality development (Lynn, 1969).

The Becker and Peterson research group reported that conduct problems were generally found in children whose parents showed poor self-control and arbitrary behavior in their interactions with their children (Becker et al., 1962; Peterson et al., 1959). In many cases, the mother was tense and thwarting while the father showed minimal concern for his family. Fathers whose children had conduct problems were frequently poor enforcers of discipline, especially of rules established by the mother. On the other hand, maladjusted and domineering fathers appeared to contribute to shyness and emotional immaturity in their children. These fathers were likely to make arbitrary power assertions and to lack warmth in dealing with their wives and children. Becker and Krug (1964) found that girls who were overly submissive and fearful often had excessively punitive and overbearing fathers. These findings are in line with those of Rubenstein and Levitt (1957) and Hoffman (1960) who emphasized the adverse effects of arbitrary paternal power assertion on the development of the child's autonomy and interpersonal maturity.

Rosenthal et al. (1962) found that inadequate fathering was associated with a number of psychological problems in children, particularly those of an antisocial nature. These investigators attempted to relate specific patterns of paternal inadequacy with certain types of childhood psychopathology. However, as with many other studies in this area, analyses were not done in terms of sex of child. Studies taking into account sex of child as well as type of paternal behavior and type of child maladjustment need to be done.

Father imitation. Sopchak (1952) and Lazowick (1955) presented findings which support the proposition that inadequate fathering is related to the development of psychological problems. Lazowick (1955) found that inadequate identification with the father was related to a high degree of manifest anxiety in undergraduate women.

Sopchak (1952) also studied college students and reported that:

Women with tendencies toward abnormality as measured by the MMPI show a lack of identification with their fathers. . . . Masculine women identify with their fathers less than feminine women . . . and identification with the father is more important in producing normal adjustment than is identification with the mother (pp. 164-165).

The well adjusted female's identification with her father seems to involve understanding and empathizing with the father rather than acting masculine or wanting to be masculine like him (as might be the case for a boy). Such an identification may also include the sharing of certain paternal values and attitudes, as long as there is no interference with the girl's development of a feminine self-concept and an expressive mode of social interaction.

Wright and Tuska (1966) compared college women who rated themselves as very feminine with those who rated themselves as only slightly feminine, or masculine. The highly feminine women had more favorable conceptions of their fathers while the unfeminine women seemed to have engaged in more imitation of their fathers' masculine behaviors. Wright and Tuska speculated that the masculine women coped with frustrating relationships with their mothers by imitating their fathers; whereas the feminine women adopted expressive role behavior by imitating their mothers' interactions with their fathers.

Inappropriate and/or inadequate fathering is a major factor in the development of homosexuality in females. In a study by Bené (1965), female homosexuals generally reported that their fathers were weak and incompetent. Kaye et al. (1967) described evidence indicating that fathers of female homosexuals, compared to control group fathers, were more often puritanical, exploitative, and feared by their daughters, as well as possessive and infantalizing. These investigators also presented data which suggest that female homosexuality is associated with a rejection of femininity during childhood. Other researchers have also found that girls who feel devalued and rejected by their fathers are more likely to become homosexual than are girls whose fathers are warm and accepting (e.g., Hamilton, 1929; West, 1967).

Poffenberger (1959) described some of the adverse effects of paternal rejection on the child's self-concept and general attitude toward life. Case studies illustrate how fathers who do not accept their daughter's femininity can have very destructive effects on their daughter's personality development (e.g., Neubauer, 1960; West, 1967). The father who wants his daughter to be the son he never had, or the father who cannot cope with feminine behavior, may compulsively reinforce masculine-type behavior in his daughter. Difficulties in the husband-wife relationship which center around sexual interactions are particularly common in such families.

If she receives adequate fathering, the probability of the girl generally imitating the father's masculine behaviors and/or spurning her femininity seems high *only* if the mother is cold and rejecting or somehow unable to express acceptance, warmth, and nurturance toward her daughter. When the father plays an active and competent masculine role in the family, his daughter is likely to imitate his nonsextyped positive attributes and develop a broad, adaptive behavioral repertoire. If the father is inadequate, his daughter may be generally limited in her social experience and not be able to fully develop her interpersonal competence. The above speculations appear to integrate and make more intelligible the results of a number of diverse studies (e.g., Ackerman, 1957; Beier & Ratzeburg, 1953; Carpenter & Eisenberg, 1935; Gray, 1959; Mussen & Rutherford, 1963).

Positive father-daughter interaction can facilitate the girl's intellectual development. There is some scattered evidence which suggests that the girl's ability to function well on particular types of cognitive tasks is facilitated by frequent and positive interaction with her father or other older males during childhood. A number of studies cited in Chapter 4 linked paternal deprivation with impaired intellectual performance, particularly in disadvantaged children. However, with the exception of a study by Landy, Rosenberg, and Sutton-Smith (1969), researchers did not include females or did not report data separately in terms of sex of child. Landy, Rosenberg, and Sutton-Smith found that college girls who had experienced a paucity of father availability in childhood had relatively low quantitative ability. Girls who have older brothers have also been found to have higher quantitative ability than girls with older sisters (e.g., Rosenberg & Sutton-Smith, 1966). Some of Heilbrun et al.'s (1967) research supports the supposition that girls who are rejected by their fathers do relatively poorly on certain difficult cognitive tasks. Interestingly, Bing (1963) discovered a positive association between the amount the father read at home and his daughter's verbal ability.

Severe psychopathology. Paternal inadequacy can be a factor in the development of severe psychopathology in the female child as well as in the male child. Unfortunately, many of the studies examining the influence of paternal deprivation on childhood psychopathology (see Chapter 4) did not include female children or did not take sex of child into account in data analyses. However, there is some research which focuses on—or specifically includes—females.

In their extensive studies, Lidz, Parker, and Cornelison (1956) reported a high incidence of inadequate fathering for both male and female schizophrenics. The fathers of the schizophrenic females were frequently observed to be in severe conflict with their wives, to contradict their wives' decisions, and to degrade their wives in front of their daughters. These fathers made rigid and unrealistic demands on their wives. Similarly, such fathers, were insensitive to their daughters' needs to develop an independent self-concept. The fathers of the schizophrenic females made attempts to manipulate and mold their daughters in terms of their own unrealistic needs. Females who formed an allegiance with a disturbed father, frequently in reaction to rejection by an unloving mother, seemed most likely to become psychotic.

Hamilton and Wahl (1948) found that almost 75 percent of the hospitalized schizophrenic women they studied had experienced some inadequacy of fathering in childhood. Prolonged father-absence, paternal rejection, and paternal abuse were very common. Baker and Holzworth (1961) compared a group of male and female adolescents who were hospitalized because of psychological disturbances with a group who were successful in their interpersonal and school adjustments. The fathers of the hospitalized group were more likely to have had social histories involving court convictions and excessive drinking than were the fathers of the successful adolescents.

However, it is important to emphasize that variations in sociocultural background may be a primary factor contributing to such findings. For example, both criminal convictions and commitment to state hospitals are more frequent for lower-class individuals than for middle-class individuals. The general economic and social deprivation that lower-class children experience seems to exacerbate the effects of paternal deprivation.

Severe psychopathology is often related to the child's constitutional predispositions and does not usually develop simply as a function of disturbed parent-child relationships. For example, the girl who is tempermentally unresponsive to affection may negatively reinforce her father's attempts to form a positive relationship with her. Similarly, if a little girl is extremely hyperactive and aggressive, it may be very difficult for her father to treat her as a female.

Summary

Interpersonal sensitivity and the ability to express affection are particularly important facets of the girl's femininity. Fathers more than mothers vary their behavior as a function of sex of child, and fathers appear to play an especially significant role in encouraging their daughters' feminine development. The father's acceptance and reinforcement of his daughter's femininity greatly facilitates the development of her self-concept.

Interaction with a masculine and competent father provides the girl with basic experiences which she can generalize to her relationships with other males. Girls who have positive relationships with their fathers are more likely to be able to obtain satisfaction in their heterosexual relationships and to achieve happiness as wives and mothers.

Father-absence and paternal deprivation can hamper the girl's personality development. Compared to girls who have had adequate fathering, father-absent girls have more difficulties in their feminine development and in their interpersonal relationships with males. Overdependency on the mother and difficulties in controlling aggressive impulses appear to be more frequent for father-absent females. Females who have experienced inadequate fathering are more likely to be homosexual than are those who have had warm affectionate relationships with their fathers. Paternal inadequacy is also a frequent concomitant of severe psychological disturbance among females.

However, other facets of family functioning, and the child's constitutional and sociocultural background, must be considered if a thorough understanding of the influence of the father-daughter relationship is to be achieved. The father-mother relationship seems to have much impact on the girl's personality development. Chronic marital conflict and inappropriate husband-wife interaction can greatly distort the child's view of heterosexual interactions. The girl may learn very unsatisfactory patterns of interacting with males, or to avoid close relationships with males. On the other hand, if the father and mother mutually satisfy and value each other, the child is much better able to learn effective interpersonal skills.

The quality of father-mother interaction is an important determinant of personality development for both boys and girls. Individuals who possess both positive masculine and positive feminine characteristics, and secure self-concepts, are most able to actualize their potential. Men who feel certain about their masculinity and are nurturant and sensitive *as well as* independent and assertive are likely to be successful interpersonally and vocationally. Similarly, women who have pride in their femininity and are independent and assertive *as well as* nurturant and sensitive can achieve interpersonal and creative fulfillment.

7

Overview and Implications

In this chapter, in addition to a description of some relatively unexplored research areas, there is a discussion of practical applications of existing knowledge relating to the father's role in personality development.

Research Directions

Knowledge concerning the father's role in personality development has come from many different fields, including anthropology, education, psychiatry, social work, and sociology, as well as from several different areas of psychology. The understanding of the effects of the father's role on personality development will proceed more meaningfully when interdisciplinary discussion and research cooperation is increased.

Much relevant data has been reviewed and many interpretations and speculations have been made. Nevertheless, many of the syntheses of existing findings discussed in this book can be viewed as hypotheses deserving more systematic investigation, rather than as established facts. A central purpose of this book is to encourage more research examining the impact of the father's role on personality development. The present discussion is an attempt to highlight some of the most important avenues for learning more about the father's role in personality development.

Methodological issues. The bulk of the research concerning parent-child relationships and personality development can be criticized because of methodological deficiencies and/or because of limited generality. In most investigations, the father's behavior is not directly assessed, and maternal or child reports of paternal behavior are used. In many of the studies, the sources of evidence about parental behavior and the child's behavior are not independent, leading to problems of interpretation. For example, in many studies the child is

119

asked to describe both his own and his parents' behavior. More studies in which there is an assessment of the amount of consistency among observer ratings of familial interactions and children's and parents' perceptions of parent-child relationships should be done. In addition, procedures which allow observers, parents, and children to rate each family member independently should be compared to those in which instructions call for comparative ratings of family members. One goal of such investigations would be to examine which type or types of measures are most related to specific dimensions of children's personality functioning.

Most of the studies done concerning the father-child relationship and personality development have been of a correlational nature. Often, the child's perception of his father or some report of the father's behavior is linked to a measure of the child's personality development. Many such studies relating to sex-role development are reviewed in Chapter 2. For instance, when significant correlations are found between the degree to which a boy perceives his father as nurturant and the boy's masculinity, it is usually assumed that paternal nurturance has been an antecedent of masculine development. But fathers may become nurturant and accepting towards their sons when their sons are masculine, and rejecting when their sons are un-masculine. Longitudinal research would be particularly helpful in determining the extent to which certain paternal behaviors precede and/or are antecedents of particular dimensions of children's behavior. Careful observations of families in various environmental settings could be especially revealing.

In addition to the obvious theoretical and practical relevance of studying the effects of father-absence, a possible methodological justification is that father-absence is a naturalistic manipulation. It can be argued that father-absence must be an antecedent rather than a consequence of certain behaviors in children. However, many researchers have treated father-absence in an overly simplistic fashion. In many studies, there has been no specification of such variables as type, length, and age of onset of father-absence. Few researchers have matched father-absent and father-present children. Potentially important variables such as sex of child, IQ, sociocultural background, birth order, sibling distrubution, and availability of father surrogates are often not taken into account, either in subject matching or in data analysis (see Chapter 1). When careful matching procedures are followed, it is interesting to note that more clear-cut findings emerge (e.g., Biller, 1969b; Hetherington, 1966).

Investigators have made inferences about the effects of father-absence and variations in paternal behavior on sex-role development and the identification process, but measurement of hypothesized dependent variables has often been indirect or included only a very narrow range of behaviors. Data concerning a limited measure of masculinity have frequently been used to make inferences concerning overall patterns of identification and sex-role development. Studies in which there has been an attempt to examine the impact of the father's role, in terms of independent measures of masculinity and of femininity, have not as yet been published. For example, it is possible that paternally deprived boys, as compared to boys who have received adequate fathering, differ more in terms of degree of femininity than in degree of masculinity. Comparisons of children with various types of fathering with respect to different facets of self-concept, expressive behavior, cognitive styles, and creativity represent some relatively unchartered but promising research areas.

Reasons for paternal deprivation. There is little systematic data indicating if the reason for paternal deprivation influences the child's personality development. In a study with fifth grade boys, Santrock and Wohlford (1970) compared boys who were father-absent as a result of their father's death with boys who were father-absent because of divorce and desertion. The boys whose fathers had died were less aggressive in doll play and were rated as less independent by their teachers than were boys who were father-absent for other reasons. However, Benson (1968) cited some research which suggests that the father's death has less of an adverse effect on the child's development than does father-absence due to divorce or separation. For instance, there is evidence that delinquency is more associated with father-absence due to separation or divorce than to father-absence due to death (Goode, 1961). In any case, more research is needed. As emphasized in Chapter 5, research taking into account the effects of variations in maternal attitudes in relation to reason for father-absence might be particularly helpful in clarifying our understanding of the father-absent child's personality development.

A related question is whether the reason for father-absence has more effect on the immediate reactions of children or on their long-term personality development. Loss of father due to death may lead to more acute behavioral reactions in children than loss of father due to other factors, but father-absence may have general effects on personality development irrespective of reason for father-absence. If the reason for father-absence has an impact on the child's personality development, much of the effect is mediated through the mother-child relationship. Researchers should also examine why, after husband absence, certain women remain unmarried or without consistent male companionship. Long-term father or father-surrogate absence as well as onset of father-absence is, in some cases, much a function of the mother's attitudes toward men.

Constitutional factors. There is much speculation in this book on ways in which the child's constitutional predispositions can affect the father-child relationship. Individual differences among both adequately fathered and paternally deprived children need to be carefully explored. Many paternally deprived boys behave in a generally effective and masculine manner. For example, an additional case-study analysis of some of the five-year-old boys in my (1968a; 1969b) studies has indicated that father-absent boys who are relatively mesomorphic are less likely to be retarded in their sex-role development than are father-absent boys with unmasculine physiques. A boy's physique has an important stimulus value in terms of the expectations and reinforcements it elicits from others and it may, along with correlated congenital factors, predispose him toward success or failure in particular types of activities. The influence of the child's anatomical, tempermental, and cognitive predispositions on parental behavior must be taken into account (e.g., Bell, 1968; Thomas et al., 1963).

Constitutional factors can have an important impact on personality development, and under certain circumstances they may be associated with inadequate fathering. Because of social and economic reasons, women who are not living with their husbands are more likely to have inadequate prenatal care. Poor prenatal care is sometimes related to neurological damage to the fetus, which in turn can contribute to deficits in the cognitive functioning of the developing child. Bronfenbrenner (1967) discusses such data when he considers the academic difficulties often encountered by the lower-class black child.

Developmental periods. The timing of fathering and father-absence is quite important. Evidence is cited in Chapter 1 which indicates that a boy's sex-role orientation is more affected by father-absence, especially if it occurs before the fifth year, than are more manifest aspects of his sex-role development. However, a long-term longitudinal investigation of father-absent children has yet to be carried out. Some of the effects of paternal deprivation during particular periods may not become apparent until the individual is much older. There is also a need for studies which take into account both period of father-absence and length of father-absence.

Our understanding of the child's personality development might be more complete if we were able to carefully examine the personality functioning of the parents before the birth of the child. The husband-wife relationship, the expectant father's attitudes towards children, and the parents' adjustment during pregnancy should be examined in terms of their possible linkage with postpartum father-child interaction. In particular, father-child interaction during the child's first few years of life should be studied in great detail.

Substitute models. Evidence reviewed in Chapter 1 indicates that surrogate models such as siblings and peers can facilitate sex-role development. Carefully planned research, exposing groups of paternally deprived children in varying degrees to father-surrogates, needs to be done. Data which are described in Chapter 2 reveal that the quality of the father-child relationship is more important than the amount of time the father is available. However, much more research concerning the influence of variations of both quantitative and qualitative paternal availability should be carried out.

There has been a lack of systematic consideration of the role of the stepfather in the child's personality development. Some investigators have found evidence suggesting that the presence of a step-father can negatively affect the child's psychological functioning (e.g., Langner and Michael, 1963). It is, of course, the quality of the stepfather-child relationship and not the presence of a stepfather per se which affects the child's personality development. The age at which the mother remarries seems to be a critical variable. For example, the young child who feels paternally deprived may find it much easier to accept a stepfather than the adolescent who may have established a strong sense of independence. Similarly, the stepfather may react more favorably to the young affectionate child than to the older child who refuses to accept his authority. The quality of the mother-child relationship and the mother's attitude toward the stepfather are also very important factors.

Types of paternal deprivation. Comparisons of children who have had ineffectual fathers with those who are father-absent are needed. There are some data which suggest that boys from father-absent homes may, in many cases, be less retarded in their masculine development than are boys from intact maternally dominated homes (Biller, 1968a). In Nye's (1957) study, children from broken homes were found to have better family adjustments, and to have lower rates of antisocial behavior and psychosomatic illness than were children from unhappy unbroken homes. Other research has also suggested that a child may function more adequately in a father-absent home than in one in which there is an inappropriate husband-wife relationship (e.g., Benson, 1968; Landis, 1962).

Father-absent children may be more influenced by factors outside the home than are children from intact but unhappy and/or maternally dominated homes. There is some evidence that father-absent children are more responsive to verbal praise than are father-present children (Phillips, 1966). Because of their intense feelings of paternal deprivation, many father-absent children are particularly affected by attention from adult males. In contrast, the father-present but inadequately fathered child is likely to develop a more negative and less flexible view of adult male behavior. For example, the father-present but maternally dominated child is prone to view men as ineffectual.

Research which is described in Chapter 4, and in other chapters, indicates that inadequate fathering and/or father-absence predisposes children toward certain developmental deficits. However, there are many paternally deprived children who are generally well adjusted. Such children should be more carefully studied, in order to determine why they differ from less well-adjusted, paternally deprived children. Investigators should include consideration of both type of paternal inadequacy and type of child maladjustment.

The mother's influence. In Chapter 5 it is speculated that the quality of the mother-child relationship is particularly important in the personality development of the paternally deprived child. Few investigators have attempted to relate individual differences in mothering to the paternally deprived child's personality development. The results of studies comparing paternally deprived individuals having different types of adjustments (e.g., neurotics, psychotics, homosexuals, generally well-functioning individuals) in terms of their relationships with their mothers might be quite revealing. Compared to mothers, fathers in intact homes seem to be more concerned with sex-typing and to more frequently base their expectations and reinforcements on the basis of sex of child. The mother's ability to facilitate the sex-role differentiation process in the father-absent or paternally deprived family is extremely crucial.

More research is needed which takes into account overall family interactions. Data are presented in this book which indicate that the husband-wife relationship is very important in influencing the father's interaction with his children. The mother's view of the father and her own sex-role development are factors which can affect the father's involvement in his family. In turn, the father's behavior has much impact on the mother's ability to rear her children. The complexity of family functioning calls for systematic observations of the ways in which various family members interact and communicate with one another.

Sociocultural factors. The significance of the family's sociocultural background has been emphasized throughout this book. In Chapters 1 and 5 there is consideration of ways in which peer group values can influence the paternally deprived boy's behavior. Chapter 3 contains a discussion of the impact of social class and the father's occupation on the father-child relationship. At several points, and particularly in Chapters 3, 4, and 5, there are speculations concerning social class differences in parent-child relationships.

Paternal deprivation seems to handicap the lower-class child more than it does the middle-class child. Paternal-absence or inadequacy adds to the generally debilitating effects experienced by the economically disadvantaged segment of our society. Paternal-absence or inadequacy is often associated with a lack of material resources. Economic deprivation can make it much more difficult for the father-absent child to avail himself of experiences which might positively affect his development. Consistent economic deprivation makes it easy to develop a defeatist attitude about one's potential impact on the environment. As Herzog and Sudia (1970) cogently pointed out, many researchers uncritically assume that a child's personality difficulties are due simply to father-absence without considering the impact of economic deprivation. However, some researchers have collected data which indicate that economically disadvantaged children suffer from paternal deprivation even when socioeconomic status is controlled (e.g., Biller, 1968b; Hetherington, 1966).

Variations in sociocultural background make the father's role more important in some societies and subgroups than in others. Cross-cultural studies combining both ecological and experimental techniques are quite valuable in increasing our knowledge of the effects of variations in family interaction on personality development. Historically focused analyses of the father's role in the family can also be very provocative and educative (e.g., Taylor, 1953).

Sex of child. As is evident from the findings reviewed in Chapter 6, a girl's as well as a boy's personality development may be negatively influenced by paternal deprivation. Some data suggest that females are less affected by father-absence than are males (e.g., Bach, 1946; Lynn & Sawrey, 1959); but there is research which supports the conclusion that girls are at least as much influenced by their relationships with their fathers as are boys (e.g., Biller & Weiss, 1970; Johnson, 1963). The extent and direction of sex differences probably varies with respect to which dimensions of personality development are considered. Much more research is needed to determine the differential impact of variations in fathering as a function of sex of child.

In any case, a warm relationship with a father who is secure in his masculinity and competent in his interpersonal relationships is a very significant factor in the sex-role and personality development of both boys and girls. Boys and girls who have interested fathers who play a positive and significant role in family interactions generally develop more adequate self-concepts and are more effective in their cognitive and interpersonal functioning than are children who have been continuously father-absent or have been inadequately fathered.

The suggestions which are discussed in this chapter are just some of the possible directions for future research. Other research avenues are explicitly or implicitly noted throughout the book. Although there have been limitations and deficiencies in most investigations relating to the effects of fathering on personality, it is possible to make definite generalizations on the basis of the seeming consistency of available data. Certain practical implications follow from the related generalizations that paternal deprivation often leads to problems in personality development, and that adequate fathering can positively influence many facets of psychological functioning.

Practical Applications

A father may be at home a great deal and yet not have much significant interaction with his children. All too often society measures a father's adequacy in terms of his income or the number of children he has sired. It is important that recognition be given to fathers who have meaningful relationships with their children.

With increased leisure time, there is a growing potential for fathers to become more involved with their children. In families which enjoy relative economic security, the father can spend much time with his children. However, many fathers seem to be much more concerned with their long-term occupational status than with their family's psychological well-being. In many families, priorities can be altered without undue economic hardship.

In families in which the father has to be away from home a great deal, the family's schedule can be arranged so that he can maximize the time he has to interact with his children. For example, if the father works in the afternoon and evening, the child can take a long nap and can be with his father at night. In any case, the family can plan many of their activities so that the father is an active participant. Even in families in which the father is very available, it is important that the child has frequent opportunities to spend time alone with him. Such occasions can be especially facilitative for sharing feelings and experiences, and in the overall strengthening of father-child communication.

A common problem in families in which there are many children is the lack of time for the parents and children to get to know one another as individuals. The ability of parents to relate to each of their children is at least as crucial as their ability to economically provide for them. This consideration should be taken into account in family planning and in more general attempts to deal with the population explosion.

The purpose of this book has not been to argue that the father is more important than the mother. The child who experiences *both positive fathering and positive mothering* is more likely to achieve effective personality functioning than the child who has only one adequate parent. Child-rearing can be a very demanding process but can be much more rewarding when the husband and wife function as a cooperative team. Together, parents often react in a more creative and responsible manner. They can be more secure in allowing their children autonomy and freedom, as well as maintaining firmness in setting necessary limits.

It is important for the child to be able to observe father-mother interaction in various situations involving the expression of emotion and problem-solving. The child can learn much from witnessing the display of mutual parental respect and understanding and the effective solution of parental disagreements. Such experiences can form the basis for the child's success in interpersonal relationships.

The consequences of paternal deprivation include disadvantages for fathers as well as children. The uninvolved father does not experience the gratification of actively facilitating the successful development of his children. He misses a meaningful opportunity to learn to deal in a sensitive way with many interpersonal situations. Widespread paternal inadequacy contributes to the existence of large numbers of interpersonally insensitive men. Many of these men are in positions of authority and their alienation as fathers has limited their ability to interact with young people. Inadequate paternal involvement is a factor in the problems of communication between individuals of different ages—contributing to the generation gap.

When the father is a peripheral member of his family, he may not have the concern for others that an involved fatherhood could help him to develop. The women's liberation movement seems, in part, a reaction to paternal deprivation. One of their key assertions is that lack of father participation has given women an unfair portion of the responsibility for child-rearing.

Psychotherapy. Since paternally deprived individuals are overrepresented among individuals with psychological problems, it is not surprising that they are found in abundance in the case reports of psychotherapists. Despite the lack of controlled research, there are many illuminating descriptions of how psychotherapists have attempted to help father-absent or inadequately fathered children (e.g., Forrest, 1966, 1967; Meerloo, 1956; Neubauer, 1960; Stoller, 1968; Wylie & Delgado, 1959).

Unfortunately, the emphasis on the mother-child relationship in most child psychotherapy has usually obscured the father's role. Rubenstein and Levitt (1957) emphasized that the father should be included in treatment considerations, but the father is often ignored or just peripherally involved. Even in the early stages of contacting an agency, the father's participation in getting help for his child seems very significant. Using standardized paper and pencil techniques, L'Abate (1960) assessed the level of emotional disturbance of mothers and children when they initially made contact with a child guidance clinic. He compared mothers and children who were accompanied by fathers with those who came without fathers. The mothers and children of families in which the father did not come to the clinic were found to be more emotionally disturbed.

Family therapy. The father should be encouraged to participate in the assessment and treatment of his child's problem. In many cases, the father's participation can be made a condition for helping the family. The importance of the father to the family and his potential for positively affecting his child should be stressed in making such demands. Even if the child's problems do not stem from inadequate fathering, the father's active involvement may do much to improve the situation. If a child has been paternally deprived, a family difficulty may provide the opportunity for getting the father more integrated into the family. It is striking how many well-meaning fathers are relatively peripheral members of their families. Many difficulties that children and mothers experience can be quickly remedied or mitigated if ways in which the father can become a more active participant are clearly communicated to the family. Much of the success of family therapy is due to the inclusion of the father (e.g., Ackerman, 1966; Forrest, 1969; Haley & Hoffman, 1967).

A child's problems, if not directly a result of family interactions, are often exacerbated by the family's reaction to them. Treating the father, mother, child, and other relevant family members as a group allows the therapist to observe both strengths and difficulties in family interactions. Valuable time can be saved and a more accurate understanding can be achieved by direct observation of family behavior rather than inferring how the family interacts from comments made by the child or his parents.

The application of modeling and related behavior modification techniques such as those described by Bandura and Walters (1963) is a particularly meaningful course to explore in individual, group, and family therapy with paternally deprived children. The probability of successful treatment can be greatly increased if knowledge concerning the process of positive fathering, and sex-role development, is integrated into the psychotherapy process. For example, the therapist can demonstrate appropriate paternal behaviors in his interactions with the family.

The therapist can explicitly model ways in which a father can communicate to his wife and to his children. Having both a male and female therapist provides even more explicit examples of appropriate male-female interactions for the family to observe. Role-playing procedures for family members are very helpful in teaching and reinforcing effective behavior patterns. Of course, any attempt to modify the family's functioning should take into account their previous modes of interaction and their sociocultural background. It is important that the family's environment is considered in treatment. Observing and modifying the family's behavior is often more meaningful when it is done in their own home rather than in the therapist's office.

Father substitutes. The availability of father surrogates is important for father-present children with inadequate fathers, as well as for father-absent children. Many paternally deprived children have very effective father surrogates in their own families or find an adequate role model among teachers or older peers. Older well-adjusted boys can be very salient and influential models for younger paternally deprived children. In cases in which it is impossible or impractical to deal with the child's father, therapists can strengthen their impact on the father-absent or paternally disadvantaged child by also working with the child's actual or potential father surrogate. This could be accomplished by consultation, but engaging the father surrogate and child in joint sessions (or in groups with other children and father surrogates) can be even more beneficial.

The Gluecks (1950) reported that many delinquent boys who form a close relationship with a father surrogate resolve their antisocial tendencies. Similarly, Trenaman (1952) found that young men who had been chronically delinquent while serving in the British army improved as a function of their relationships with father surrogates. A paternally deprived boy may be particularly responsive to a male therapist or role model because of his motivation for male companionship. Rexford (1964), in describing the treatment of young antisocial children, noted that therapists are more likely to be successful with father-absent boys than with boys who have strongly identified with an emotionally disturbed, criminal, or generally inadequate father.

There are many organizations including Big Brother, Y.M.C.A., Boy Scouts, athletic teams, camps, churches, and settlement houses which provide paternally deprived children with meaningful father surrogates. Additional professional consultation and more community support (especially more father surrogates), would allow these organizations to be of even greater benefit to many more children.

Available research indicates that even in the first few years of life, the child's personality development can be very much influenced by the degree and type of involvement of a father or father surrogate. Group settings such as Head Start and day care centers can be used as vehicles to provide father surrogates for those children (both boys and girls) who could profit from them. The facilities of such organizations as Big Brother and the Y.M.C.A. could also be utilized to help younger children.

Education. Nursery schools, kindergartens, and elementary schools would have a greater positive influence on children if more male teachers were available (e.g., McCandless, 1967; Ostrovsky, 1959). Male teachers might be able to facilitate certain types of cognitive functioning in paternally deprived children as well as contributing to their interpersonal development. There is a need for incentives to encourage more males to become teachers of young children. However, our school systems could better utilize already available teachers.

Many of the men whose teaching is now confined to the upper elementary school grades could also be very effective with younger children. Opportunities can be developed for male teachers to spend some of their time with a greater range of children, or children who are particularly father-deprived. Similarly, other males such as older students or retired men can also be invited to interact with young children in our schools as well as in other settings.

Community mental health. Children confined to institutions are especially in need of warm relationships with competent father surrogates. Institutionalized children, including those who are orphaned or emotionally disturbed, can benefit from a larger proportion of interaction with adult males. For example, Nash's (1965) data suggest that having institutionalized children live in a situation in which they are cared for and supervised by a husband-wife team is beneficial for their sex-role development. Keller and Alper (1970) have contributed many guidelines for adult males working with delinquent children in institutional settings and halfway houses.

Prospective fathers and father surrogates can be made more aware of the significance of the father in child development through education and the mass media. Potentially, such exposure along with other programs can lessen the number of families which become father-absent. Explicit advantages, such as financial and other support for fathers remaining with their families, in contrast to the current rewarding of father-absence by many welfare departments, might do much to keep some families intact and reconstitute other families.

Preventive programs can focus on families which seem to have a high risk of becoming father-absent. Systematic techniques can be developed to determine the potential consequences of father-absence for a family where separation or divorce is being contemplated. There are many families in which both the parents and the children would be able to function better subsequent to divorce. It also seems that, when the divorce process is taking place, more consideration should be given to whether all or some of the children might benefit from remaining with their fathers. It is usually easier to find mother surrogates (e.g., grandmothers, housekeepers) than to find father surrogates. It is also relevant to consider potential paternal effectiveness in placing children with adoptive or foster parents.

Applications of existing knowledge should not be divorced from research endeavors. Treatment and preventive projects can be integrated with research programs. Baker et al. have provided an excellent example of research designed to suggest answers to practical issues concerning paternal deprivation (Baker et al., 1967; 1968; Fagen et al., 1967). They carried out a short-term longitudinal investigation of the families of army professionals. Their findings have clearly detailed some of the complexities of family adjustment to 1) anticipated father-absence (first phase of assessment, one to three months before father's departure); 2) temporary father-absence (second phase of assessment, six to nine months after father had left); and 3) the father's reunion with his family (third phase of assessment, at least six months after the father had returned). Although extensive assessment procedures were used, the age of the boys at the time of father-absence (six- and seven-years-old), the relatively short duration of father-absence, and the seemingly significant prefather-absent differences among families made it difficult to find any consistent personality differences directly attributable to father-absence. However, the Baker et al. research project has made important contributions by delineating individual differences in modes of family adjustment to father-absence, and by leading to specific suggestions concerning the use of family and community resources to alleviate crisis situations concerning father-absence.

The mother in the paternally deprived family must not be neglected. For example, the mother's reaction to husband-absence may greatly influence the extent to which father-absence or lack of father availability affects her children. She is often in need of psychological as well as social and economic support. Mental health professionals have outlined many useful techniques for helping mothers and children in fatherless families (e.g., Baker et al., 1968; Despert, 1957; Hill, 1949; Lerner, 1954; McDermott, 1968; Wylie & Delgado, 1959).

In a pilot project, one of the central goals of a welfare mothers' group was to help husbandless mothers constructively deal with their social and familial problems (Biller & Smith, 1972). Pollak

(1971) discussed the frequent interpersonal and sexual problems of spouseless parents and gave some excellent suggestions for helping such parents cope with their concerns. Education and therapeutic groups such as "Parents Without Partners" can be very meaningful for the wifeless father as well as the husbandless mother (e.g., Freudenthal, 1959; Schlesinger, 1966).

A significant dimension of community mental health efforts, both in terms of prevention and treatment, should be supplying father surrogates to groups of paternally deprived children. Far-reaching community, state, and government programs are needed. A vast number of children do not have consistent and meaningful contact with adult males. This very serious situation must be remedied if all our children are to take full advantage of their growing social and educational opportunities.

References

References

Aberle, D.F. & Naegele, F.D. Middle-class fathers' occupational role and attitude toward children. *American Journal of Orthopsychiatry,* 1952, *22,* 366-378.

Ackerman, N.W. The principle of shared responsibility of child rearing. *International Journal of Sociology,* 1957, *12,* 280-291.

Ackerman, N.W. *Treating the troubled family.* New York: Basic Books, 1966.

Aichorn, A. *Wayward Youth.* New York: Viking Press, 1935.

Albert, R.S. Early cognitive development among the gifted. Paper presented at the meeting of the Western Psychological Association, Vancouver, British Columbia, Canada, June, 1969.

Aldous, J. Children's perceptions of adult roles as affected by class, father absence, and race. *DARCEE Papers and Reports,* 1969, *4,* No. 3.

Alkire, A.A. Social power and communication within families of disturbed and nondisturbed preadolescents. *Journal of Personality and Social Psychology,* 1969, *13,* 335-349.

Altucher, N. Conflict in sex identification in boys. Unpublished doctoral dissertation, University of Michigan, 1957.

Altus, W.D. The broken home and factors of adjustment. *Psychological Reports,* 1958, *4,* 477.

Anastasiow, N.S. Success in school and boys' sex-role patterns. *Child Development,* 1965, *36,* 1053-1066.

Ancona, L., Cesa-Bianchi, M., & Bocquet, C. Identification with the father in the absence of the paternal model. Research applied to children of Navy officers. *Archivo di Psicologia Neurologia e Psichiatria,* 1964, *24,* 339-361.

Anderson, L.M. Personality characteristics of parents of neurotic, aggressive, and normal preadolescent boys. *Journal of Consulting and Clinical Psychology*, 1969, *33*, 575-581.

Anderson, R.E. Where's Dad? Paternal deprivation and delinquency. *Archives of General Psychiatry*, 1968, *18*, 641-649.

Andrews, R.O. & Christensen, H.T. Relationship of absence of a parent to courtship status: A repeat study. *American Sociological Review*, 1951, *16*, 541-544.

Andry, R.G. Paternal and maternal roles in delinquency. In *Deprivation of maternal care*. Public Health Paper No. 14. Geneva: World Health Organization, 1962, 31-43.

Angrilli, A.F. The psychosexual identification of preschool boys. *Journal of Genetic Psychology*, 1960, *97*, 329-340.

Bach, G.R. Father-fantasies and father typing in father-separated children. *Child Development*, 1946, *17*, 63-80.

Bach, G.R. & Bremer, G. Projective father fantasies of preadolescent delinquent children. *Journal of Psychology*, 1947, *24*, 3-17.

Bacon, M.K., Child, I.L. & Barry, H. III. A cross-cultural study of correlates of crime. *Journal of Abnormal and Social Psychology*, 1963, *66*, 291-300.

Baker, J.W., & Holzworth, A. Social histories of successful and unsuccessful children. *Child Development*, 1961, *32*, 135-149.

Baker, S.L., Cove, L.A., Fagen, S.A., Fischer, E.G., & Janda, E.J. Impact of father-absence: III. Problems of family reintegration following prolonged father-absence. Paper presented at the meeting of the American Orthopsychiatric Association, Washington, D.C., March, 1968.

Baker, S.L., Fagen, S.A., Fischer, E.G., Janda, E.J., & Cove, L.A. Impact of father-absence on personality factors of boys: I. An evaluation of the military family's adjustment. Paper presented at the meeting of the American Orthopsychiatric Association, Washington, D.C., March 1967.

Baldwin, A.L., Kalhorn, J., & Breese, F.A. The appraisal of parent behavior. *Psychological Monographs,* 1949, *63,* No. 1 (Whole No. 299).

Bandura, A., Ross, D. & Ross, S.A. A comparative test of the status envy, social power, and secondary reinforcement theories of identificatory learning. *Journal of Abnormal and Social Psychology,* 1963, *67,* 527-534.

Bandura, A. & Walters, R.H. Dependency conflicts in aggressive delinquents. *Journal of Social Issues,* 1958, *14,* 52-65.

Bandura, A. & Walters, R.H. *Adolescent aggression: A study of the influence of child-rearing practices and family interrelationships.* New York: Ronald Press, 1959.

Bandura, A. & Walters, R.H. *Social learning and personality development.* New York: Holt, Rinehart, & Winston, 1963.

Barclay, A.G. & Cusumano, D. Father-absence, cross-sex identity, and field-dependent behavior in male adolescents. *Child Development,* 1967, *38,* 243-250.

Barry, H. III, Bacon, M.K., & Child, I.L. A cross-cultural survey of some sex differences in socialization. *Journal of Abnormal and Social Psychology,* 1957, *55,* 327-332.

Bartemeir, L. The contribution of the father to the mental health of the family. *American Journal of Psychiatry,* 1953, *110,* 277-280.

Baruch, D.W. & Wilcox, J.A. A study of sex differences in preschool children's adjustment coexistent with interparental tensions. *Journal of Genetic Psychology,* 1944, *61,* 281-303.

Baumrind, D. & Black, A.E. Socialization practices associated with dimensions of competence in preschool boys and girls. *Child Development,* 1967, *38,* 291-327.

Baxter, J.C., Horton, D.L., & Wiley, R.E. Father identification as a function of the mother-father relationship. *Journal of Individual Psychology,* 1964, *20,* 167-171.

Beck, A.T., Sehti, B.B., & Tuthill, R.W. Childhood bereavement and adult depression. *Archives of General Psychiatry,* 1963, *9,* 295-302.

Becker, W.C. Consequences of different kinds of parental discipline. In M.L. Hoffman & L.W. Hoffman (Eds.), *Review of Child Development Research: Vol. I.* New York: Russell Sage Foundation, 1964, 169-208.

Becker, W.C. & Krug, R.S. A circumplex model for social behavior in children. *Child Development,* 1964, *35,* 371-396.

Becker, W.C., Peterson, D.R., Luria, Z., Shoemaker, D.S., & Hellmer, L.A. Relations of factors derived from parent interview ratings to behavior problems of five-year-olds. *Child Development,* 1962, *33,* 509-535.

Beier, E.G. & Ratzeburg, F. The parental identifications of male and female college students. *Journal of Abnormal and Social Psychology,* 1953, *48,* 569-572.

Bell, R.Q. A reinterpretation of the direction of effects of studies of socialization. *Psychological Review,* 1968, *75,* 81-95.

Beller, E.K. Maternal behaviors in lower-class Negro mothers. Paper presented at the meeting of the Eastern Psychological Association, Boston, April, 1967.

Bené, E. On the genesis of female homosexuality. *British Journal of Psychiatry,* 1965, *3,* 815-821.

Benjamin, H. Age and sex differences in the toy preferences of young children. *Journal of Genetic Psychology*, 1932, *41*, 417-429.

Benson, L. *Fatherhood: A sociological perspective.* New York: Random House, 1968.

Berry, J.W. Temne and Eskimo perceptual skills. *International Journal of Psychology*, 1966, *1*, 207-229.

Bieber, I., et al. *Homosexuality: A psychoanalytic study.* New York: Basic Books, 1962.

Bieliauskas, V. Recent advances in the psychology of masculinity and femininity. *Journal of Psychology*, 1965, *60*, 255-263.

Bieri, J. Parental identification, acceptability, and authority, and within sex-differences in cognitive behavior. *Journal of Abnormal and Social Psychology*, 1960, *60*, 76-79.

Bieri, J. & Lobeck, R. Acceptance of authority and parental identification. *Journal of Personality*, 1959, *27*, 74-87.

Biller, H.B. A multiaspect investigation of masculine development in kindergarten-age boys. *Genetic Psychology Monographs*, 1968, *76*, 89-139. (a)

Biller, H.B. A note on father-absence and masculine development in young lower-class Negro and white boys. *Child Development*, 1968, *39*, 1003-1006. (b)

Biller, H.B. Father dominance and sex-role development in kindergarten-age boys. *Developmental Psychology*, 1969, *1*, 87-94. (a)

Biller, H.B. Father-absence, maternal encouragement, and sex-role development in kindergarten age boys. *Child Development*, 1969, *40*, 539-546. (b)

Biller, H.B. Maternal salience and feminine development in young girls. *Proceedings of the 77th Annual Convention of the American Psychological Association,* 1969, *4,* 259-260. (c)

Biller, H.B. Father-absence and the personality development of the male child. *Developmental Psychology,* 1970, *2,* 181-201.

Biller, H.B. The mother-child relationship and the father-absent boy's personality development. *Merrill-Palmer Quarterly,* 1971, *17,* 227-241.

Biller, H.B. & Bahm, R.M. Father-absence, perceived maternal behavior, and masculinity of self-concept among junior high school boys. *Developmental Psychology,* 1971, *4,* 178-181.

Biller, H.B. & Barry, W. Sex role patterns, paternal similarity, and personality adjustment in college males. *Developmental Psychology,* 1971, *4,* 107.

Biller, H.B. & Borstelmann, L.J. Intellectual level and sex-role development in mentally retarded children. *American Journal of Mental Deficiency,* 1965, *70,* 443-447.

Biller, H.B. & Borstelmann, L.J. Masculine development: An integrative review. *Merrill-Palmer Quarterly,* 1967, *13,* 253-294.

Biller, H:B. & Liebman, D.A. Body build, sex-role preference, and sex-role adoption in junior high school boys. *Journal of Genetic Psychology,* 1971, *118,* 81-86.

Biller, H.B. & Poey, K. An exploratory comparison of sex-role related behavior in schizophrenics and nonschizophrenics. *Developmental Psychology,* 1969, *1,* 629.

Biller, H.B., Singer, D.L., & Fullerton, M. Sex-role development and creative potential in kindergarten-age boys. *Developmental Psychology,* 1969, *1,* 291-296.

Biller, H.B., & Smith, A.E. An AFDC mothers group: An exploratory effort in community mental health. *Family Coordinator*, 1972, in press.

Biller, H.B. & Weiss, S. The father-daughter relationship and the personality development of the female. *Journal of Genetic Psychology*, 1970, *114*, 79-93.

Bing, E. Effect of child-rearing practices on development of differential cognitive abilities. *Child Development*, 1963, *34*, 631-648.

Birdwhistell, R.L. Is there an ideal father? *Child Study*, 1957, *34*, 29-33.

Blanchard, R.W. & Biller, H.B. Father availability and academic performance among third-grade boys. *Developmental Psychology*, 1971, *4*, 301-305.

Blood, R.O., Jr. & Wolfe, D.M. *Husbands and Wives: The dynamics of married living.* New York: Free Press, 1960.

Bloom, B. & Arkoff, A. Role-playing in acute and chronic schizophrenia. *Journal of Consulting Psychology*, 1961, *25*, 24-28.

Bowerman, C.E. & Elder, G.H., Jr. Variations in adolescent perception of family power structure. *American Sociological Review*, 1964, *29*, 551-567.

Brigham, J.C., Ricketts, J.L., & Johnson, R.C. Reported maternal and paternal behaviors of solitary and social delinquents. *Journal of Consulting Psychology*, 1967, *31*, 420-422.

Brill, N.Q. & Liston, E.H., Jr. Parental loss in adults with emotional disorders. *Archives of General Psychiatry*, 1966, *14*, 307-314.

Brim, O.G. Family structure and sex-role learning by children: A further analysis of Helen Koch's data. *Sociometry*, 1958, *21*, 1-16.

Bronfenbrenner, U. The study of identification through interpersonal perception. In R. Tagiuri & L. Petrullo (Eds.) *Person perception and interpersonal behavior.* Stanford: Stanford University Press, 1958, 110-130.

Bronfenbrenner, U. Freudian theories of identification and their derivatives. *Child Development,* 1960, *31,* 15-40.

Bronfenbrenner, U. Some familial antecedents of responsibility and leadership in adolescents. In L. Petrullo & B.M. Bass (Eds.), *Leadership and interpersonal behavior.* New York: Holt, Rinehart, and Winston, 1961, 239-272.

Bronfenbrenner, U. The psychological costs of quality and equality in education. *Child Development,* 1967, *38,* 909-925.

Bronson, W.C. Dimensions of ego and infantile identification. *Journal of Personality,* 1959, *27,* 532-545.

Brown, D.G. Sex-role preference in young children. *Psychological Monographs,* 1956, *70,* No. 14, (Whole No. 421).

Brown, D.G. Sex-role development in a changing culture. *Psychological Bulletin,* 1958, *55,* 232-241.

Brown, D.G. Sex-role preference in children: Methodological problems. *Psychological Reports,* 1962, *11,* 477-478.

Brown, D.G. & Tolor, A. Human figure drawings as indicators of sexual identification and inversion. *Perceptual and Motor Skills,* 1957, *7,* 199-211.

Burgess, E.W. & Locke, H.J. *The Family.* New York: American Book Company, 1953.

Burton, R.V. & Whiting, J.W.M. The absent father and cross-sex identity. *Merrill-Palmer Quarterly,* 1961, *7,* 85-95.

Busse, T.W. Child-rearing antecedents of flexible thinking. *Developmental Psychology,* 1969, *1,* 585-591.

Carlsmith, L. Effect of early father-absence on scholastic aptitude. *Harvard Educational Review*, 1964, *34*, 3-21.

Carpenter, J. & Eisenberg, P. Some relations between family background and personality. *Journal of Psychology*, 1935, *6*, 115-136.

Cava, E.L. & Rausch, H.L. Identification and the adolescent boy's perception of his father. *Journal of Abnormal and Social Psychology*, 1952, *47*, 855-856.

Cervantes, L.F. Family background, primary relationships, and the high school dropout. *Journal of Marriage and The Family*, 1965, *27*, 218-223.

Cheek, F.E. A serendipitous finding: Sex roles and schizophrenia. *Journal of Abnormal and Social Psychology*, 1964, *69*, 392-400.

Clausen, J.A. Family structure, socialization, and personality. In L.W. Hoffman & M.L. Hoffman (Eds.), *Review of child development research, Vol. 2.* New York: Russell Sage Foundation, 1966, 1-53.

Cobb, H.V. Role wishes and general wishes of children and adolescents. *Child Development*, 1954, *60*, 392-400.

Cobliner, W.G. Social factors in mental disorders: A contribution to the etiology of mental illness. *Genetic Psychology Monographs*, 1963, *67*, 151-215.

Colley, T. The nature and origin of psychological sexual identity. *Psychological Review*, 1959, *66*, 165-177.

Coopersmith, S. *The antecedents of self-esteem.* San Francisco: W.H. Freeman, 1967.

Cottrell, L.S. The adjustment of the individual to his age and sex roles. *American Sociological Review*, 1942, *7*, 617-620.

Cox, F.N. An assessment of children's attitudes towards parent figures. *Child Development*, 1962, *33*, 821-830.

146

Crain, A.J. & Stamm, C.S. Intermittent absence of fathers and children's perceptions of parents. *Journal of Marriage and the Family,* 1965, *27,* 344-347.

Crane, A.R. A note on preadolescent gangs. *Australian Journal of Psychology,* 1951, *3,* 43-46.

Crane, A.R. Preadolescent gangs: a sociopsychological interpretation. *Journal of Genetic Psychology,* 1955, *86,* 275-279.

Crites, J.O. Parental identification in relation to vocational interest development. *Journal of Educational Psychology,* 1962, *53,* 262-270.

Dai, B. Some problems of personality development among Negro children. In C. Kluckhohn, H.A. Murray, & D.M. Schneider (Eds.), *Personality in nature, society, and culture.* New York: Knopf, 1953, 545-566.

D'Andrade, R.G. Father-absence and cross-sex identification. Unpublished doctoral dissertation, Harvard University, 1962.

D'Andrade, R.G. Sex differences and cultural institutions. In E.E. Maccoby (Ed.), *The Development of Sex Differences.* Stanford: Stanford University Press, 1966, 174-204.

Da Silva, G. The role of the father with chronic schizophrenic patients. *Journal of the Canadian Psychiatric Association,* 1963, *8,* 190-203.

Davis, A. & Havighurst, R.J. Social class and color differences in child rearing. *American Sociological Review,* 1946, *11,* 698-710.

DeLucia, L.A. The toy preference test: A measure of sex-role identification. *Child Development,* 1963, *34,* 107-117.

Dennehy, C. Childhood bereavement and psychiatric illness. *British Journal of Psychiatry,* 1966, *112,* 1049-1069.

Despert, L.J. The fatherless family. *Child Study,* 1957, *34,* 22-28.

Deutsch, H. *The Psychology of Women, Vol. I.*, New York: Grune & Stratton, 1944.

Deutsch, M. Minority group and class status as related to social and personality factors in scholastic achievement. *Monograph of the Society for Applied Anthropology,* 1960, *2,* 1-32.

Deutsch, M. & Brown, B. Social influences in Negro-white intelligence differences. *Journal of Social Issues,* 1964, *20,* 24-35.

Devereux, E.C., Jr., Bronfenbrenner, U., & Suci, G.J. Patterns of parent behavior in the United States and the Federal Republic of Germany: A cross-national comparison. *International Social Science Journal,* 1962, *14,* 488-506.

Diamond, S. *Personality and Temperment.* New York: Harper & Row, 1957.

Dinitz, S., Dynes, R.R., & Clarke, A.C. Preferences for male or female children: traditional or affectional. *Marriage and Family Living,* 1954, *16,* 128-130.

Distler, L.S. Patterns of parental identification: An examination of three theories. Unpublished doctoral dissertation, University of California, Berkeley, 1964.

Domini, G.P. An evaluation of sex-role identification among father-absent and father-present boys. *Psychology,* 1967, *4,* 13-16.

Douvan, E. & Adelson, J. *The adolescent experience.* New York, Wiley, 1966.

Downey, K.J. Parental interest in the institutionalized, severely mentally retarded child. *Social Problems,* 1963, *11,* 186-193.

DuHamel, T.R. & Biller, H.B. Parental imitation and nonimitation in young children. *Developmental Psychology,* 1969, *1,* 772.

Dyk, R.B. & Witkin, H.A. Family experiences related to the development of differentiation in children. *Child Development,* 1965, *36,* 21-55.

Eisenberg, L. The fathers of autistic children. *American Journal of Orthopsychiatry,* 1957, *27,* 715-725.

Elder, G.H., Jr. *Adolescent achievement and mobility aspirations.* Chapel Hill, N.C.: Institute for Research in Social Science, 1962.

Elder, G.H., Jr. & Bowerman, C.E. Family structure and child-rearing patterns: The effect of family size and sex composition. *American Sociological Review,* 1963, *28,* 891-905.

Emmerich, W. Parental identification in young children. *Genetic Psychology Monographs,* 1959, *60,* 257-308.

Engel, I.M. A factor-analytic study of five masculinity-femininity tests. *Journal of Consulting Psychology,* 1966, *30,* 565.

Erikson, E.H. Identity and the life cycle. *Psychological Issues,* 1959, *1,* (Whole No. 1).

Eron, L.D., Walder, L.O., Toigo, R. & Lefkowitz, M.M. Social class, parental punishment for aggression, and child aggression. *Child Development,* 1963, *34,* 849-867.

Fagen, S.A., Janda, E.J., Baker, S.L., Fischer, E.G. & Cove, L.A. Impact of father-absence in military families: II. Factors relating to success of coping with crisis. Paper presented at the meeting of the American Psychological Association, Washington, D.C., September, 1967.

Fagot, B.I. & Patterson, G. An in vivo analysis of reinforcing contingencies for sex-role behaviors in the preschool child. *Developmental Psychology,* 1969, *1,* 563-568.

Farber, B. Effects of a severely mentally retarded child on the family.

In E.P. Trapp & P. Himelstein (Eds.), *Readings on the exceptional child.* New York: Appleton-Century Crofts, 1962, 227-246.

Farina, A. Patterns of role-dominance and conflict in parents of schizophrenic patients. *Journal of Abnormal and Social Psychology,* 1960, *61,* 31-38.

Fauls, L.B. & Smith, W.P. Sex-role learning of five-year-olds. *Journal of Genetic Psychology,* 1956, *89,* 105-117.

Fenichel, O. *The Psychoanalytic Theory of Neurosis.* New York: Norton, 1945.

Fish, K.D. Paternal availability, family role-structure, maternal employment, and personality development in late adolescent females. Unpublished doctoral dissertation, University of Massachusetts, 1969.

Fish, K.D. & Biller, H.B. Perceived childhood paternal relationships and college females' personal adjustment. *Adolesence,* 1972, in press.

Fleck, S., Lidz, T., & Cornelison, A. A comparison of parent-child relationships of male and female schizophrenic patients. *Archives of General Psychiatry,* 1963, *8,* 1-7.

Forrest, T. Paternal roots of female character development. *Contemporary Psychoanalyst,* 1966, *3,* 21-28.

Forrest, T. The paternal roots of male character development. *The Psychoanalytic Review,* 1967, *54,* 81-99.

Forrest, T. Treatment of the father in family therapy. *Family Process,* 1969, *8,* 106-117.

Foster, J.E. Father images: Television and ideal. *Journal of Marriage and the Family,* 1964, *26,* 353-355.

Franck, K. & Rosen, E.A. A projective test of masculinity-femininity. *Journal of Consulting Psychology*, 1949, *13*, 247-256.

Frazier, E.F. *The Negro Family in the United States.* Chicago: University of Chicago Press, 1939.

Freedheim, D.K. An investigation of masculinity and parental role patterns. Unpublished doctoral dissertation, Duke University, 1960.

Freedheim, D.K. & Borstelmann, L.J. An investigation of masculinity and parental role-patterns. *American Psychologist,* 1963, *18,* 339. (Abstract)

Freud, A. & Burlington, D.T. *Infants without families.* New York: International University Press, 1944.

Freud, S. The passing of the Oedipus complex. *Collected papers, Vol. II.* London: Hogarth Press, 1924.

Freud S. *New Introductory Lectures in Psychoanalysis.* New York: Norton, 1933.

Freud, S. *Leonardo Da Vinci: A study in psychosexuality.* New York: Random House, 1947.

Freud, S. Some psychological consequences of the anatomical distinction between the sexes. In *Collected papers, Vol. V.* London: Hogarth Press, 1950, 186-197.

Freud, S. Group psychology and the analysis of the ego. In J. Strachey (Ed.), *The Complete Psychological Works of Sigmund Freud Vol 1.* London: Hogarth Press, 1955, 69-143.

Freudenthal, K. Problems of the one-parent family. *Social Work,* 1959, *4,* 44-48.

Garai, J.E. & Scheinfeld, A. Sex differences in mental and behavioral traits. *Genetic Psychology Monographs,* 1968, *77,* 169-299.

Garbower, G. *Behavior problems of children in navy officers' families: As related to social conditions of Navy family life.* Washington, D.C.: Catholic University Press, 1959.

Gardiner, G.E. Separation of the parents and the emotional life of the child. In S. Glueck (Ed.), *The Problems of Delinquency.* Boston: Houghton-Mifflin, 1959, 138-143.

Gardner, G.G. The relationship between childhood neurotic symptomatology and later schizophrenia in males and females. *Journal of Nervous and Mental Disease,* 1967, *144,* 97-100.

Garn, S.M. & Clark, L.C., Jr. The sex difference in the basal metabolic rate. *Child Development,* 1953, *24,* 215-224.

Garn, S.M. Fat, body size, and growth in the newborn. *Human Biology,* 1958, *30,* 265-280.

Gay, M.J. & Tonge, W.L. The late effects of loss of parents in childhood, *British Journal of Psychiatry,* 1967, *113,* 753-759.

Gerard, D.L. & Siegal, J. The family background of schizophrenia. *Psychiatric Quarterly,* 1950, *24,* 47-73.

Glasser, P. & Navarre, E. Structural problems of the one-parent family. *Journal of Social Issues,* 1965, *21,* 98-109.

Glueck, S. & Glueck, E. *Unravelling Juvenile Delinquency.* New York: Commonwealth Fund, 1950.

Glueck, S. & Glueck, E. *Physique and delinquency.* New York: Harper & Row, 1956.

Gold, M. & Slater, C. Office, factory, store—and family: A study of integration setting. *American Sociological Review,* 1958, *23,* 64-74.

Goldberg, S. & Lewis, M. Play behavior in the year-old infant. Early sex differences. *Child Development,* 1969, *40,* 21-31.

152

Goldin, P.C. A review of children's reports of parent behaviors. *Psychological Bulletin,* 1969, *71,* 222-236.

Goode, W. Family disorganization. In R.K. Merton & R.A. Nisbet (Eds.), *Contemporary Social Problems.* New York: Harcourt, Brace, & World, 1961.

Goodenough, E.W. Interest in persons as an aspect of sex differences in the early years. *Genetic Psychology Monographs,* 1957, *55,* 287-323.

Gorer, G. *The American People: A study of national character.* New York: Norton, 1948.

Gover, D.A. Socioeconomic differential in the relationship between marital adjustment and wife's employment status. *Marriage and Family Living,* 1963, *25,* 452-458.

Gray, S.W. Masculinity-femininity in relation to anxiety and social acceptance. *Child Development,* 1957, *28,* 203-214.

Gray, S.W. Perceived similarity to parents and adjustment. *Child Development,* 1959, *30,* 91-107.

Gray, S.W. & Klaus, R. The assessment of parental identification. *Genetic Psychology Monographs,* 1956, *54,* 87-114.

Green, A.W. The middle-class child and neurosis. *American Sociological Review,* 1946, *11,* 31-41.

Greenstein, J.F. Father characteristics and sex-typing. *Journal of Personality and Social Psychology,* 1966, *3,* 271-277.

Gregory, I. Studies of parental deprivation in psychiatric patients. *American Journal of Psychiatry,* 1958, *115,* 432-442.

Gregory, I. Anterospective data following childhood loss of a parent:

I. Delinquency and high school dropout. *Archives of General Psychiatry*, 1965, *13*, 99-109. (a)

Gregory, I. Anterospective data following childhood loss of a parent: II. Pathology, performance, and potential among college students. *Archives of General Psychiatry*, 1965, *13*, 110-120. (b)

Grønseth, E. The impact of father-absence in sailor families upon the personality structure and social adjustment of adult sailor sons, part I. In N. Anderson (Ed.), *Studies of the family, Vol. 2*. Gottingen: Vandenhoeck & Ruprecht, 1957, 97-114.

Grunebaum, M.G., Hurwitz, I., Prentice, N.M. & Sperry, B.M. Fathers of sons with primary neurotic learning inhibition. *American Journal of Orthopsychiatry*, 1962, *32*, 462-473.

Gundlach, R.H. Childhood parental relationships and the establishment of gender roles of homosexuals. *Journal of Consulting and Clinical Psychology*, 1969, *33*, 136-139.

Haley, J. & Hoffman, L. *Techniques of family therapy*. New York: Basic Books, 1967.

Hall, M. & Keith, R.A. Sex-role preference among children of upper- and lower-social class. *Journal of Social Psychology*, 1964, *62*, 101-110.

Hall, P. & Tonge, W.L. Long-standing continuous unemployment in male patients with psychiatric symptoms. *British Journal of Preventive and Social Medicine*, 1963, *17*, 191-196.

Hamburg, D.A. & Lunde, D.T. Sex hormones in the development of sex differences in human behavior. In E.E. Maccoby (Ed.), *The Development of sex differences*. Stanford: Stanford University Press, 1966, 1-24.

Hamilton, C.V. *A research in marriage*. New York: Boni, 1929.

Hamilton, D.M. & Wahl, J.G. The hospital treatment of dementia praecox. *American Journal of Psychiatry,* 1948, *105,* 346-352.

Hampson, J.L. Determinants of psychosexual orientation. In F.A. Beach (Ed.), *Sex and Behavior.* New York: Wiley, 1965, 108-132.

Hardy, M.C. Aspects of home environment in relation to behavior at the elementary school age. *Journal of Juvenile Research,* 1937, *21,* 206-225.

Harlow, R.G. Masculine inadequacy and compensatory development of physique. *Journal of Personality,* 1951, *19,* 312-333.

Hartley, R.E. Sex-role pressures and socialization of the male child. *Psychological Reports,* 1959, *5,* 457-468.

Hartley, R.E. The one-parent family. In *Reference papers on children and youth.* 1960 White House Conference on Children and Youth.

Hartley, R.E. A developmental view of female sex-role definition and identification. *Merrill-Palmer Quarterly,* 1964, *10,* 3-16.

Hartley, R.E., & Klein, A. Sex-role concepts among elementary-school -age girls. *Marriage and Family Living,* 1959, *21,* 59-64.

Hartup, W.W. Some correlates of parental imitation in young children. *Child Development,* 1962, *33,* 85-96.

Hartup, W.W. & Zook, E.A. Sex-role preference in three- and four-year-old children. *Journal of Consulting Psychology,* 1960, *24,* 420-426.

Haworth, M.R. Parental loss in children as reflected in projective responses. *Journal of Projective Techniques,* 1964, *28,* 31-35.

Heckel, R.V. The effects of fatherlessness on the preadolescent female. *Mental Hygiene,* 1963, *47,* 69-73.

Heckscher, B.T. Household structure and achievement orientation in lower-class Barbadian families. *Journal of Marriage and the Family,* 1967, *29,* 521-526.

Heilbrun, A.B. Parental identification and college adjustment. *Psychological Reports,* 1962, *10,* 853-854.

Heilbrun, A.B. The measurement of identification. *Child Development,* 1965, *36,* 111-127. (a)

Heilbrun, A.B. An empirical test of the modeling theory of sex-role learning. *Child Development,* 1965, *36,* 789-799. (b)

Heilbrun, A.B. & Fromme, D.K. Parental identification of late adolescents and level of adjustment: the importance of parent-model attributes, ordinal position, and sex of child. *Journal of Genetic Psychology,* 1965, *107,* 49-59.

Heilbrun, A.B., Harrell, S.N., & Gillard, B.J. Perceived childrearing attitudes of fathers and cognitive control in daughters. *Journal of Genetic Psychology,* 1967, *111,* 29-40.

Helper, M.M. Learning theory and the self-concept. *Journal of Abnormal and Social Psychology,* 1955, *51,* 184-194.

Herzog, E, & Sudia, C.E. *Boys in fatherless families.* Washington: U.S. Department of Health, Education, and Welfare, Office of Child Development, Children's Bureau, 1970.

Hetherington, E.M. A developmental study of the effects of sex of the dominant parent on sex-role preference, identification, and imitation in children. *Journal of Personality and Social Psychology,* 1965, *2,* 188-194.

Hetherington, E.M. Effects of paternal absence on sex-typed behaviors in Negro and white preadolescent males. *Journal of Personality and Social Psychology,* 1966, *4,* 87-91.

Hetherington, E.M. & Brackbill, Y. Etiology and covariation of obstinacy, orderliness, and parsimony in young children. *Child Development*, 1963, *34*, 919-943.

Hetherington, E.M. & Frankie, G. Effects of parental dominance, warmth, and conflict on imitation in children. *Journal of Personality and Social Psychology*, 1967, *6*, 119-125.

Hilgard, J.R., Neuman, M.F. & Fisk, F. Strength of adult ego following bereavement. *American Journal of Orthopsychiatry*, 1960, *30*, 788-798.

Hill, J.P. Similarity and accordance between parents and sons in attitudes towards mathematics. *Child Development*, 1967, *38*, 777-791.

Hill, O.W. & Price, J.S. Childhood bereavement and adult depression. *British Journal of Psychiatry*, 1967, *113*, 743-751.

Hill, R. *Families under stress.* New York: Harper, 1949.

Hoffman, L.W. The father's role in the family and the child's peer-group adjustment. *Merrill-Palmer Quarterly*, 1961, *7*, 97-105.

Hoffman, M.L. Power assertion by the parent and its impact on the child. *Child Development*, 1960, *31*, 129-143.

Hoffman, M.L. Father absence and conscience development. *Developmental Psychology*, 1971, *4*, 400-406.

Holman, P. Some factors in the etiology of maladjustment in children. *Journal of Mental Science*, 1953, *99*, 654-688.

Hooker, E. Parental relations and male homosexuality in patient and nonpatient samples. *Journal of Consulting and Clinical Psychology*, 1969, *33*, 140-142.

Ingham, H.V. A statistical study of family relationships in psycho-neurosis. *American Journal of Orthopsychiatry*, 1949, *106*, 91-98.

Jacobson, G. & Ryder, R.G. Parental loss and some characteristics of the early marriage relationship. *American Journal of Ortho-psychiatry*, 1969, *39*, 779-787.

Johnson, M.A. & Meadow, A. Parental identification among male schizophrenics. *Journal of Personality*, 1966, *34*, 300-309.

Johnson, M.M. Sex-role learning in the nuclear family. *Child Develop-ment*, 1963, *34*, 319-333.

Kagan, J. Socialization of aggression and the perception of parents in fantasy. *Child Development*, 1958, *29*, 311-320. (a)

Kagan, J. The concept of identification. *Psychological Review*, 1958, *65*, 296-305. (b)

Kagan, J. Acquisition and significance of sex typing and sex-role identity. In M.L. Hoffman & L.W. Hoffman (Eds.), *Review of Child Development Research, Vol. 1.* New York: Russell Sage Foundation, 1964, 137-167.

Kagan, J. & Moss, H. *Birth to Maturity.* New York: Wiley, 1962.

Kardiner, A. & Ovesey, L. *The Mark of Oppression.* New York: Norton, 1951.

Kaye, H.E., et al. Homosexuality in women. *Archives of General Psychiatry*, 1967, *17*, 626-634.

Kayton, R. & Biller, H.B. Perception of parental sex-role behavior and psychopathology in adult males. *Journal of Consulting and Clinical Psychology*, 1971, *36*, 235-237.

Kayton, R. & Biller, H.B. Sex-role development and psychopathology in adult males. *Journal of Consulting and Clinical Psychology,* 1972, *38,* 308-310.

Kaufman, I., Peck, A.I., & Tagiuri, C.K. The family constellation and overt incestuous relations between father and daughter. *American Journal of Orthopsychiatry,* 1954, *24,* 266-277.

Keeler, W.R. Children's reaction to the death of a parent. In P.H. Hoch & J. Zubin (Eds.), *Depression.* New York: Grune, 1954, 109-120.

Keller, O.J., Jr. & Alper, B.S. *Halfway houses: Community-centered correction and treatment.* Lexington, Mass.: Heath-Lexington Books, D.C. Heath, 1970.

Kimball, B. The Sentence Completion Technique in a study of scholastic underachievement. *Journal of Consulting Psychology,* 1952, *16,* 353-358.

King, C.E. The Negro maternal family: A product of an economic and culture system. *Social Forces,* 1945, *24,* 100-104.

Kluckhohn, C. *Mirror for man.* New York: McGraw-Hill, 1949.

Knop, C.A. The dynamics of newly born babies. *Journal of Pediatrics,* 1946, *29,* 721-728.

Koch, H.L. Sissiness and tomboyishness in relation to sibling characteristics. *Journal of Genetic Psychology,* 1956, *88,* 231-244.

Koch, M.B. Anxiety in preschool children from broken homes. *Merrill-Palmer Quarterly,* 1961, *1,* 225-231.

Kohlberg, L. A cognitive-developmental analysis of children's sex-role concepts and attitudes. In E.E. Maccoby (Ed.), *The development of sex differences.* Stanford: Stanford University Press, 1966, 82-173.

Kohlberg, L. & Zigler, E. The impact of cognitive maturity on the development of sex-role attitudes in the years four-eight. *Genetic Psychology Monographs,* 1967, *75,* 89-165.

Kragh, U. & Kroon, T. An analysis of aggression and identification in young offenders by the study of perceptual development. *Human Development,* 1966, *9,* 209-221.

Kriesberg, L. Rearing children for educational achievement in father-less families. *Journal of Marriage and the Family,* 1967, *29,* 288-301.

L'Abate, L. The effect of paternal failure to participate during the referral of child psychiatric patients. *Journal of Clinical Psychology,* 1960, *16,* 407-408.

La Barre, W. *The human animal.* Chicago: University of Chicago Press, 1954.

Landy, F., Rosenberg, B.G., & Sutton-Smith, B. The effect of limited father-absence on the cognitive and emotional development of children. Paper presented at the meeting of the Midwestern Psychological Association, Chicago, May, 1967.

Landy, F., Rosenberg, B.G., & Sutton-Smith, B. The effect of limited father-absence on cognitive development. *Child Development,* 1969, *40,* 941-944.

Landis, J.T. The trauma of children when parents divorce. *Marriage and Family Living,* 1960, *22,* 7-13.

Landis, J.T. A reexamination of the role of the father as an index of family integration. *Marriage and Family Living,* 1962, *24,* 122-128.

Langner, T.S. & Michael, S.T. *Life stress and mental health.* New York: Free Press, 1963.

Lansky, L.M. Patterns of defense against conflict. Unpublished doctoral dissertation. University of Michgan, 1956.

Lansky, L.M. The family structure also affects the model: Sex-role attitudes in parents of preschool children. *Merrill-Palmer Quarterly,* 1967, *13,* 139-150.

Lansky, L.M. & McKay, G. Sex-role preferences of kindergarten boys and girls: Some contradictory results. *Psychological Reports,* 1963, *13,* 415-421.

Lawton, M.J. & Sechrest, L. Figure drawings by young boys from father-present and father-absent homes. *Journal of Clinical Psychology,* 1962, *18,* 304-305.

Layman, E.M. Discussion. In D.G. Applezweig (Chm.) Childhood and mental health: The influence of the father in the family setting. Symposium presented at the American Psychological Association, Chicago, September, 1960 (Reprinted in *Merrill-Palmer Quarterly,* 1961, *1,* 107-111).

Lazowick, L.M. On the nature of identification. *Journal of Abnormal and Social Psychology,* 1955, *51,* 175-183.

Lederer, W. Dragons, delinquents, and destiny. *Psychological Issues,* 1964, *4,* (Whole No. 3).

Lefkowitz, M.M. Some relationships between sex-role preference of children and other parent and child variables. *Psychological Reports,* 1962, *10,* 43-53.

Leichty, M.M. The effect of father-absence during early childhood upon the Oedipal situation as reflected in young adults. *Merrill-Palmer Quarterly,* 1960, *6,* 212-217.

Leiderman, G.F. Effect of family experiences on boys' peer relationships. Unpublished doctoral dissertation, Harvard University, 1953.

Leiderman, G.F. Effect of parental relationships and child-training practices on boys' interactions with peers. *Acta Psychologica,* 1959, *15,* 469.

Leonard, M.R. Fathers and daughters. *International Journal of Psychoanalysis,* 1966, *47,* 325-333.

Lerner, S.H. Effect of desertion on family life. *Social Casework,* 1954, *35,* 3-8.

Levin, H. & Sears, R.R. Identification with parents as a determinant of doll play aggression. *Child Development,* 1956, *37,* 135-153.

Levin, R.B. An empirical test of the female castration complex. *Journal of Abnormal Psychology,* 1966, *71,* 181-188.

Levy, D.M. *Maternal overprotection.* New York: Columbia University Press, 1943.

Lidz, T., Fleck, S. & Cornelison, A.R. *Schizophrenia and the human family.* New York: International Universities Press, 1965.

Lidz, T., Parker, N. & Cornelison, A.R. The role of the father in the family environment of the schizophrenic patient. *American Journal of Psychiatry,* 1956, *13,* 126-132.

Linton, R. *The study of man.* New York: Appleton-Century Crofts, 1936.

Lipsitt, L.P. & Levy, N. Pain threshold in the human neonate. *Child Development,* 1959, *30,* 547-554.

Lipsitt, P.D. & Strodbeck, F.L. Defensiveness in decisionmaking as a function of sex-role identification. *Journal of Personality and Social Psychology,* 1967, *6,* 10-15.

Lipton, E.L., Steinschneider, A., & Richmond, J.B. Psychophysiologic disorders in children. In L.W. Hoffman & M.L. Hoffman (Eds.), *Review of Child Development Research, Vol. 2.* New York: Russell Sage Foundation, 1966, 169-220.

Loeb, J. The personality factor in divorce. *Journal of Consulting Psychology,* 1966, *30,* 562.

Loeb, J. & Price, J.R. Mother and child personality characteristics related to parental marital status in child guidance cases. *Journal of Consulting Psychology,* 1966, *30,* 112-117.

Luckey, E.B. Marital satisfaction and parental concept. *Journal of Consulting Psychology,* 1960, *24,* 195-204.

Lynn, D.B. A note on sex differences in the development of masculine and feminine identification. *Psychological Review,* 1959, *66,* 126-135.

Lynn, D.B. Sex differences in identification development. *Sociometry,* 1961, *24,* 372-383.

Lynn, D.B. Sex-role and parental identification. *Child Development,* 1962, *33,* 555-564.

Lynn, D.B. *Parental and sex-role identification.* Berkeley: McCutchan 1969.

Lynn, D.B. & Sawrey, W.L. The effects of father-absence on Norwegian boys and girls. *Journal of Abnormal and Social Psychology,* 1959, Vol. 59, 258-262.

MacArthur, R. Sex differences in field dependence for the Eskimo: replication of Berry's findings. *International Journal of Psychology,* 1967, *2,* 139-140.

MacDonald, M.W. Criminal behavior in passive, effeminate boys. *American Journal of Orthopsychiatry,* 1938, *8,* 70-78.

McCandless, B.R. *Children: Behavior and development.* New York: Holt, Rinehart, & Winston, 1967.

McClelland, D.C. *The achieving society.* New Jersey: Van Nostrand, 1961.

163

McClelland, D.C. & Watt, N.F. Sex-role alienation in schizophrenia. *Journal of Abnormal Psychology*, 1968, *73*, 226-239.

McCord, J., McCord, W. & Howard, A. Family interaction as an antecedent to the direction of male aggressiveness. *Journal of Abnormal and Social Psychology*, 1963, *66*, 239-242.

McCord, J., McCord, W., & Thurber, E. Some effects of paternal absence on male children. *Journal of Abnormal and Social Psychology*, 1962, *64*, 361-369.

McDermott, J.F. Parental divorce in early childhood. *American Journal of Psychiatry*, 1968, *124*, 1424-1432.

McKinley, D.G. *Social class and family life.* New York: Free Press, 1964.

Maccoby, E.E. (Ed.), *The development of sex differences.* Stanford: Stanford University Press, 1966.

Maccoby, E.E. & Rau, L. Differential cognitive abilities. Final report, U.S. Office of Education, Cooperative Research Project No. 1040, 1962.

Machover, K. *Personality projection in the drawing of the human figure.* Springfield, Illinois: Charles C. Thomas, 1949.

Madow, L. & Hardy, S.E. Incidence and analysis of the broken family in the background of neurosis. *American Journal of Orthopsychiatry*, 1947, *17*, 521-528.

Maxwell, A.E. Discrepancies between the pattern of abilities for normal and neurotic children. *Journal of Mental Science*, 1961, *107*, 300-307.

Mead, M. *Sex and temperment in three primitive societies.* New York: Morrow, 1935.

Medinnus, G.N. Delinquents' perception of their parents. *Journal of Consulting Psychology,* 1965, *29,* 5-19.

Meerloo, J.A.M. The father cuts the cord: The role of the father as initial transference figure. *American Journal of Psychotherapy,* 1956, *10,* 471-480.

Miller, B. Effects of father-absence and mother's evaluation of father on the socialization of adolescent boys. Unpublished doctoral dissertation, Columbia University, 1961.

Miller, D.R. & Swanson, G.E., et al. *Inner conflict and defense.* New York: Holt, 1960.

Miller, W.B. Lower-class culture as a generating milieu of gang delinquency. *Journal of Social Issues,* 1958, *14,* 5-19.

Mischel, W. Preference for delayed reinforcement: An experimental study of cultural observation. *Journal of Abnormal and Social Psychology,* 1958, *56,* 57-61.

Mischel, W. Preference for delayed reward and social responsibility. *Journal of Abnormal and Social Psychology,* 1961, *62,* 1-7. (a)

Mischel, W. Delay of gratification, need for achievement, and acquiescence in another culture. *Journal of Abnormal and Social Psychology,* 1961, *62,* 543-552. (b)

Mischel, W. Father-absence and delay of gratification. *Journal of Abnormal and Social Psychology,* 1961, *62,* 116-124. (c)

Mischel, W. A social learning view of sex differences in behavior. In E.E. Maccoby (Ed.), *The development of sex differences.* Stanford: Stanford University Press, 1966, 56-81.

Mishler, E.G. & Waxler, N.E. *Interaction in families.* New York: Wiley, 1968.

Mitchell, D. & Wilson, W. Relationship of father-absence to masculinity and popularity of delinquent boys. *Psychological Reports,* 1967, *20,* 1173-1174.

Monahan, T.P. Family status and the delinquent child. *Social Forces,* 1957, *35,* 250-258.

Money, J. Psychosexual differentiation. In J. Money, (Ed.), *Sex research: New developments.* New York: Holt, Rinehart & Winston, 1965, 3-23.

Moulton, P.W., Burnstein, E., Liberty, D. & Altucher, N. The patterning of parental affection and dominance as a determinant of guilt and sex-typing. *Journal of Personality and Social Psychology,* 1966, *4,* 363-365.

Mowrer, O.H. Identification: A link between learning theory and psychotherapy. In *Learning theory and personality dynamics.* New York: Ronald Press, 1950, 573-616.

Moynihan, D.P. *The Negro Family: The case for national action.* Washington, D.C.: United States Department of Labor, 1965.

Murdock, G.P. Comparative data on the division of labor by sex. *Social Forces,* 1936, *15,* 551-553.

Mumbauer, C.C. Resistance to temptation in young Negro children in relation to sex of the subject, sex of the experimenter, and father-absence or presence. *DARCEE Papers and Reports,* 1969, *3,* No. 2.

Mussen, P.H. Some antecedents and consequences of masculine sex-typing in adolescent boys. *Psychological Monographs,* 1961, *75,* No. 2 (Whole No. 506).

Mussen, P.H. Long-term consequents of masculinity of interests in adolescence. *Journal of Consulting Psychology,* 1962, *26,* 435-440.

Mussen, P.H., Conger, J.J., & Kagan, J. *Child development and personality.* New York: Harper & Row, 1969.

Mussen, P.H. & Distler, L. Masculinity, identification, and father-son relationships. *Journal of Abnormal and Social Psychology,* 1959, *59,* 350-356.

Mussen, P.H. & Distler, L. Child-rearing antecedents of masculine identification in kindergarten boys. *Child Development,* 1960, *31,* 89-100.

Mussen, P.H. & Jones, M.C. The behavior-inferred motivation of late and early maturing boys. *Child Development,* 1957, *28,* 243-256.

Mussen, P.H. & Parker, A.L. Mother nurturance and the girls' incidental imitative learning. *Journal of Personality and Social Psychology,* 1965, *2,* 94-97.

Mussen, P.H. & Rutherford, E. Parent-child relationships and parental personality in relation to young children's sex-role preferences. *Child Development,* 1963, *34,* 589-607.

Mussen, P.H., Young, H.B., Gaddini, R. & Morante, L. The influence of father-son relationships on adolescent personality and attitudes. *Journal of Child Psychology and Psychiatry,* 1963, *4,* 3-16.

Mutimer, D., Loughlin, L. & Powell, M. Some differences in the family relationships of achieving and underachieving readers. *Journal of Genetic Psychology,* 1966, *109,* 67-74.

Nash, J. The father in contemporary culture and current psychological literature. *Child Development,* 1965, *36,* 261-297.

Nelson, E.A. & Maccoby, E.E. The relationship between social development and differential abilities on the scholastic aptitude test. *Merrill-Palmer Quarterly,* 1966, *12,* 269-289.

Neubauer, P.B. The one-parent child and his Oedipal development. *Psychoanalytic Studies of the Child,* 1960, *15,* 286-309.

Norton, A. Incidence of neurosis related to maternal age and birth-order. *British Journal of Social Medicine,* 1952, *6,* 253-258.

Nye, F.I. Child adjustment in broken and unhappy unbroken homes. *Marriage and Family Living,* 1957, *19,* 356-361.

Nye, F.I. *Family relationships and delinquent behavior.* New York: Wiley, 1958.

Nye, F.I. Employment status of mothers and adjustment of adolescent children. *Marriage and Family Living,* 1959, *21,* 240-244.

O'Connor, P.J. Aetiological factors in homosexuality as seen in R.A.F. psychiatric practice. *British Journal of Psychiatry,* 1964, *110,* 381-391.

Oltman, J.E., McGarry, J.J. & Friedman, S. Parental deprivation and the 'broken home' in dementia praecox and other mental disorders. *American Journal of Psychiatry,* 1952, *108,* 685-694.

Ostrovsky, E.S. *Father to the child: Case studies of the experiences of a male teacher.* New York: Putnam, 1959.

Palmer, R.C. Behavior problems of children in Navy officers' families. *Social Casework,* 1960, *41,* 177-184.

Papenek, M.L. Authority and sex roles in the family. *Journal of Marriage and the Family,* 1969, *31,* 88-96.

Parker, S. & Kleiner, R.J. Characteristics of Negro mothers in single-headed households. *Journal of Marriage and the Family,* 1966, *28,* 507-513.

Parsons, T. Family structure and the socialization of the child. In T. Parsons & R.F. Bales (Eds.), *Family, socialization and interaction process.* Glencoe, Illinois: Free Press, 1955, 25-131.

Parsons, T. Social structure and the development of personality:

Freud's contribution to the integration of psychology and sociology. *Psychiatry,* 1958, *21,* 321-340.

Payne, D.E. & Mussen, P.H. Parent-child relations and father-identification among adolescent boys. *Journal of Abnormal and Social Psychology,* 1956, *52,* 358-362.

Pedersen, F.A. Relationships between father-absence and emotional disturbance in male military dependents. *Merrill-Palmer Quarterly,* 1966, *12,* 321-331.

Pedersen, F.A. & Rabson, K.S. Father participation in infancy. *American Journal of Orthopsychiatry,* 1969, *39,* 466-472.

Peterson, D.R., Becker, W.C., Hellmer, L.A., Shoemaker, D.J. & Quay, H.C. Parental attitudes and child adjustment. *Child Development,* 1959, *30,* 119-130.

Pettigrew, T.F. *A profile of the Negro American.* Princeton: Van Nostrand, 1964.

Phelan, H.M. The incidence and possible significance of the drawing of female figures by sixth-grade boys in response to the Draw-A-Person Test. *Psychiatric Quarterly,* 1964, *38,* 1-16.

Phillips, J. Performance of father-present and father-absent southern Negro boys on a simple operant task as a function of race and sex of the experimenter and the type of social reinforcement. Unpublished doctoral dissertation, University of Minnesota, 1966.

Piety, K.R. Patterns of parent perceptions among neuropsychiatric patients and normal controls. *Journal of Clinical Psychology,* 1967, *23,* 428-433.

Pinter, R. & Fortano, G. Some measures of dominance in college women. *Journal of Social Psychology,* 1944, *19,* 303-315.

Poffenberger, T.A. A research note on father-child relations and father viewed as a negative figure. *Child Development,* 1959, *30,* 489-492.

Poffenberger, T.A. & Norton, D. Factors in the formation of attitudes towards mathematics. *Journal of Educational Research,* 1959, *52,* 171-176.

Pollak, G.K. Sexual dynamics of parents without partners. *Social Work,* 1970, *15,* 79-85.

Pope, B. Socioeconomic contrasts in children's peer culture prestige values. *Genetic Psychology Monographs,* 1953, *48,* 157-200.

Rabban, M. Sex-role identification in young children in two diverse social groups. *Genetic Psychology Monographs,* 1950, *42,* 81-158.

Rabin, A.I. Some psychosexual differences between Kibbutz and non-Kibbutz Israeli boys. *Journal of Projective Techniques,* 1958, *22,* 328-332.

Rainwater, L. Crucible of identity. *Daedalus,* 1966, *95,* 172-216.

Rainwater, L. & Yancey, W.L. *The Moynihan Report and the politics of controversy.* Cambridge, Mass.: M.I.T. Press, 1967.

Rexford, E.N. Antisocial young children and their families. In M.R. Haworth (Ed.), *Child psychotherapy.* New York: Basic Books, 1964, 58-63.

Risen, M.L. Relation of lack of one or both parents to school progress. *Elementary School Journal,* 1939, *39,* 528-531.

Robey, A., Rosenwald, R.J., Snell, J.E., & Lee, R.E. The runaway girl: A reaction to family stress. *American Journal of Orthopsychiatry,* 1964, *34,* 762-767.

Robins, E., Schmidt, E.H., & O'Neal, P. Some interrelations of social factors and clinical diagnosis in attempted suicide. *American Journal of Psychiatry,* 1957, *114,* 221-231.

Rohrer, J.H. & Edmonson, M.S. *The eighth generation.* New York: Harper, 1960.

Romney, A.K. Variations in household structure as determinants of sex-typed behavior. In F. Beach, (Ed.), *Sex and behavior.* New York: Wiley, 1965, 208-220.

Rosen, B.C. & D'Andrade, R. The psychosocial origins of achievement motivation. *Sociometry,* 1959, *22,* 185-218.

Rosenberg, B.G. & Sutton-Smith, B. The measurement of masculinity and femininity in children. *Child Development,* 1959, *30,* 373-380.

Rosenberg, B.G. & Sutton-Smith, B. The measurement of masculine-feminine differences in play activities. *Journal of Genetic Psychology,* 1960, *96,* 165-170.

Rosenberg, B.G. & Sutton-Smith, B. Ordinal position and sex-role identification. *Genetic Psychology Monographs,* 1964, *70,* 297-328.

Rosenberg, B.G. & Sutton-Smith, B. Sibling association, family size, and cognitive abilities. *Journal of Genetic Psychology,* 1966, *107,* 271-279.

Rosenberg, B.G. & Sutton-Smith, B. Family interaction effects on masculinity-femininity. *Journal of Personality and Social Psychology,* 1968, *8,* 117-120.

Rosenberg, M. *Society and the adolescent self-image.* Princeton: Princeton University Press, 1965.

Rosenkrantz, P., Vogel, S., Bee, J., Broverman, I., & Broverman, D.M. Sex-role stereotypes and self-concepts in college students. *Journal of Consulting and Clinical Psychology,* 1968, *32,* 287-295.

Rosenthal, M.S., Ni, E., Finkelstein, M. & Berkwits, G.K. Father-child relationships and children's problems. *Archives of General Psychiatry,* 1962, *7,* 360-373.

Roth, J., & Peck, R.F. Social class and social mobility factors related to marital adjustment. *American Sociological Review,* 1951, *16,* 478-487.

Rothbart, M.K. & Maccoby, E.E. Parents' differential reactions to sons and daughters. *Journal of Personality and Social Psychology,* 1966, *4,* 237-243.

Rouman, J. School children's problems as related to parental factors. *Journal of Educational Research,* 1956, *50,* 105-112.

Rowntree, G. Early childhood in broken families. *Population Studies,* 1955, *8,* 247-253.

Rubenstein, B.O. & Levitt, M. Some observations regarding the role of fathers in child psychotherapy. *Bulletin of the Menninger Clinic,* 1957, *21,* 16-27.

Rushing, W.A. Adolescent-parent relationships and mobility aspirations. *Social Forces,* 1964, *43,* 157-166.

Russell, I.L. Behavior problems of children from broken and intact homes. *Journal of Educational Sociology,* 1957, *31,* 124-129.

Rutherford, E.E. A note on the relation of parental dominance to children's ability to make sex-role discriminations. *Journal of Genetic Psychology,* 1969, *114,* 185-191.

Rutherford, E.E. & Mussen, P.H. Generosity in nursery school boys. *Child Development,* 1968, *39,* 755-765.

Rychlak, J. & Legerski, A. A sociocultural theory of appropriate sexual role identification and level of personality adjustment. *Journal of Personality,* 1967, *35,* (1), 31-49.

Salzman, L. Psychology of the female: A new look. *Archives of General Psychiatry,* 1967, *17,* 195-203.

Sanford, N. The dynamics of identification. *Psychological Review,* 1955, *62,* 106-118.

Santrock, J.W. Paternal absence, sex-typing, and identification. *Developmental Psychology,* 1970, *2,* 264-272. (a)

Santrock, J.W. Influence of onset and type of paternal absence on the first four Eriksonian developmental crises. *Developmental Psychology,* 1970, *3,* 273-274. (b)

Santrock, J.W. & Wohlford, P. Effects of father absence: Influences of reason for, and onset of absence. *Proceedings of the 78th Annual Convention of the American Psychological Association,* 1970, *5,* 265-266.

Schlesinger, B. The one-parent family: An overview. *Family Life Coordinator,* 1966, *15,* 133-137.

Schoeppe, A., Haggard, E.A., & Havighurst, R.J. Some factors affecting sixteen-year-olds' success in five developmental tasks. *Journal of Abnormal and Social Psychology,* 1953, *48,* 42-52.

Schuham, A.I. Power relations in emotionally disturbed and normal family triads. *Journal of Abnormal Psychology,* 1970, *75,* 30-37.

Sears, P.S. Doll-play aggression in normal young children: Influence of sex, age, sibling status, father's absence. *Psychological Monographs,* 1951, *65,* No. 6.

Sears, P.S. Child-rearing factors related to playing of sex-typed roles. *American Psychologist,* 1953, *8,* 431 (Abstract).

Sears, R.R. Identification as a form of behavior development. In D.B. Harris (Ed.), *The concept of development.* Minneapolis: University of Minnesota Press, 1957, 149-161.

Sears, R.R., Maccoby, E.E. & Levin, H. *Patterns of child rearing.* Evanston, Illinois: Row, Peterson, 1957.

Sears, R.R., Pintler, M.H., & Sears, P.S. Effect of father-separation on preschool children's doll-play aggression. *Child Development,* 1946, *17,* 219-243.

Sears, R.R., Rau, L., & Alpert, R. *Identification and child rearing.* Stanford: Stanford University Press, 1965.

Seder, J.A. The origin of differences in extent of independence in children: Developmental factors in perceptual field dependence. Unpublished doctoral dissertation, Radcliffe College, 1957.

Seltzer, C.C. The relationship between the masculine component and personality. In C. Kluckhohn & H.A. Murray, (Eds.), *Personality in nature, society, and culture.* New York: Knopf, 1948, 84-96.

Seplin, C.D. A study of the influence of the father's absence for military service. *Smith College Studies in Social Work,* 1952, *22,* 123-124.

Seward, G.H. Cultural conflict and the feminine role: An experimental study. *Journal of Social Psychology,* 1945, *22,* 177-194.

Seward, G.H. *Sex and the social order.* New York: McGraw-Hill, 1946.

Shaw, M.C. & White, D.L. The relationship between child-parent identification and academic underachievement. *Journal of Clinical Psychology,* 1965, *21,* 10-13.

Sheldon, W.H. Constitutional factors in personality. In J. McV. Hunt (Ed.), *Personality and the behavior disorders.* New York: Ronald Press, 1944, 526-549.

Sherman, R.C. & Smith, F. Sex differences in cue-dependency as a function of socialization environment. *Perceptual and Motor Skills,* 1967, *24,* 599-602.

Shortell, J.R. & Biller, H.B. Aggression in children as a function of sex of subject and sex of opponent. *Developmental Psychology*, 1970, *3*, 143-144.

Siegman, A.W. Father-absence during childhood and antisocial behavior. *Journal of Abnormal Psychology*, 1966, *71*, 71-74.

Slocum, W.L. & Stone, C.L. Family culture patterns and delinquent type behavior. *Marriage and Family Living*, 1963, *25*, 202-208.

Smelser, W.T. Adolescent and adult occupational choice as a function of family socioeconomic history. *Sociometry*, 1963, *4*, 393-409.

Sopchak, A.L. Parental "identification" and tendency toward disorder as measured by the MMPI. *Journal of Abnormal and Social Psychology*, 1952, *47*, 159-165.

Stanfield, R.E. The interaction of family variables and gang variables in the aetiology of delinquency. *Social Problems*, 1966, *13*, 411-417.

Steimel, R.J. Childhood experiences and masculinity-femininity scores. *Journal of Consulting Psychology*, 1960, *7*, 212-217.

Stendler, C.B. Critical periods in socialization and overdependency. *Child Development*, 1952, *23*, 3-12.

Stendler, C.B. Possible causes of overdependency in young children. *Child Development*, 1954, *25*, 125-146.

Stephens, W.N. Judgments by social workers on boys and mothers in fatherless families. *Journal of Genetic Psychology*, 1961, *99*, 59-64.

Stephens, W.N. *The Oedipus complex: Cross-cultural evidence.* Glencoe, Illinois: Free Press, 1962.

Stoke, S.M. An inquiry into the concept of identification. *Journal of Genetic Psychology,* 1950, *76,* 164-184.

Stoller, R.J. *Sex and gender.* New York: Science House, 1968.

Stolz, L.M., et al. *Father relations of war-born children.* Stanford: Stanford University Press, 1954.

Strodtbeck, F.L. Family interaction, values, and achievement. In D.C. McClelland et al. (Eds.), *Talent and Society,* New York: Van Nostrand, 1958, 135-194.

Suedfield, P. Paternal absence and overseas success of Peace Corps volunteers. *Journal of Consulting Psychology,* 1967, *31,* 424-425.

Sunley, R. Early nineteenth-century American literature on child-rearing. In M. Mead and M. Wolfenstein (Eds.), *Childhood in contemporary cultures.* Chicago: University of Chicago Press, 1955.

Sutherland, H.E.G. The relationship between I.Q. and size of family in the case of fatherless children. *Journal of Genetic Psychology,* 1930, *38,* 161-170.

Sutton-Smith, B, Roberts, J.M., & Rosenberg, B.G. Sibling associations and role involvement. *Merrill-Palmer Quarterly,* 1964, *10,* 25-38.

Sutton-Smith, B., & Rosenberg, B.G. Age changes in the effects of ordinal position on sex role identification. *Journal of Genetic Psychology,* 1965, *107,* 61-73.

Sutton-Smith, B., Rosenberg, B.G., & Landy, F. Father-absence effects in families of different sibling compositions. *Child Development,* 1968, *38,* 1213-1221.

Swenson, C.H. & Newton, K.R. The development of sexual differentiation on the Draw-A-Person Test, *Journal of Clinical Psychology,* 1955, *11,* 417-419.

Tallman, I. Spousal role differentiation and the socialization of severely retarded children. *Journal of Marriage and the Family,* 1965, *27,* 37-42.

Tasch, R.J. The role of the father in the family. *Journal of Experimental Education,* 1952, *20,* 319-361.

Tasch, R.J. Interpersonal perceptions of fathers and mothers. *Journal of Genetic Psychology,* 1955, *87,* 59-65.

Taylor, G.R. *Sex in history.* London: Thames and Hudson, 1953.

Terman, L.M. & Miles, C.C. *Sex and personality.* New York: McGraw-Hill, 1936.

Terman, L.M. & Oden, M.H. *The gifted child grows up.* Stanford: Stanford University Press, 1947.

Thomas, A., Chess, S., Birch, H.G., Hertzig, M.E., & Korn, S. *Behavioral individuality in early childhood.* New York: New York University Press, 1963.

Thomes, N.M. Children with absent fathers. *Journal of Marriage and the Family,* 1968, *30,* 89-96.

Thrasher, F.M. *The Gang.* Chicago: University of Chicago Press, 1927.

Tiller, P.O. Father-absence and personality development of children in sailor families. *Nordisk Psyckologi's Monograph Series,* 1958, *9,* 1-48.

Tiller, P.O. *Father separation and adolescence.* Oslo, Norway: Institute for Social Research, 1961.

Toby, J. The differential impact of family disorganization. *American Sociological Review,* 1957, *22,* 505-512.

Torgoff, I. & Dreyer, A.S. Achievement inducing and independence granting-synergistic parental role components: Relation to daughter's "parental" role orientation and level of aspiration. *American Psychologist,* 1961, *16,* 345, (Abstract).

Travis, J. Precipitating factors in manic-depressive psychoses. *Psychiatric Quarterly,* 1933, *8,* 411-418.

Trenaman, J. *Out of step.* London: Methuen, 1952.

Tuckman, J. & Regan, R.A. Intactness of the home and behavioral problems in children. *Journal of Child Psychology and Psychiatry,* 1966, *7,* 225-233.

Tuddenham, R.D. Studies in reputation: III. Correlates of popularity among elementary school children. *Journal of Educational Psychology,* 1951, *42,* 257-276.

Tuddenham, R.D. Studies in reputation: I. Sex and grade differences in school children's evaluations of their peers. II. The diagnosis of social adjustment. *Psychological Monographs,* 1952, *66,* (Whole No. 333).

Tyler, L.E. The relationship of interests to abilities and reputation among first-grade children. *Educational Psychology Measurement,* 1951, *11,* 255-264.

Veroff, J., Atkinson, J., Feld, S., & Gurin, G. The use of thematic apperception to assess motivation in a nationwide interview study. *Psychological Monographs,* 1960, *74,* (Whole No. 499).

Vogel, S.R., et al. Maternal employment and perception of sex roles among college students. *Developmental Psychology,* 1970, *3,* 384-391.

Vroegh, K., Jenkin, N., Black, M., & Hendrick, M. Discriminant analysis of preschool masculinity and femininity. *Multivariate Behavioral Research,* 1967, *2,* 299-313.

Wahl, C.W. Antecedent factors in family histories of 392 schizophrenics. *American Journal of Psychiatry,* 1954, *110,* 668-676.

Wahl, C.W. Some antecedent factors in the family histories of 568 male schizophrenics of the U.S. Navy. *American Journal of Psychiatry,* 1956, *113,* 201-210.

Walker, R.N. Body-build and behavior in young children: I. Body-build and nursery school teachers' ratings. *Monograph of the Society for Research in Child Development,* 1962, *27,* No. 3 (Serial No. 84).

Walker, R.N. Body-build and behavior in young children: II. Body-build and parents' ratings. *Child Development,* 1963, *34,* 1-23.

Warren, W. & Cameron, K. Reactive psychosis in adolescence, *Journal of Mental Science,* 1950, *96,* 448-457.

Webb, A.P. Sex-role preferences and adjustment in early adolescents. *Child Development,* 1963, *34,* 609-618.

West, D.J. Parental relationships in male homosexuality. *International Journal of Social Psychiatry,* 1959, *5,* 85-97.

West, D.J. *Homosexuality.* Chicago: Aldine, 1967.

White, B. The relationship of self-concept and parental identification to women's vocational interests. *Journal of Consulting Psychology,* 1959, *6,* 202-206.

White, R.W. Competence and the psychosexual stages of development. In M.R. Jones (Ed.), *Nebraska Symposium on Motivation,* 1960, Lincoln: University of Nebraska Press, 1960, 97-141.

Whiting, J.W.M. Sorcery, sin, and the superego: A cross-cultural study of some mechanisms of social control. In M.R. Jones (Ed.), *Nebraska Symposium on Motivation,* 1959, Lincoln: University of Nebraska Press, 1959, 174-195.

Whiting, J.W.M., Kluckhohn, R., & Anthony, A. The function of male initiation ceremonies at puberty. In E.E. Maccoby, T.M. Newcomb, & E.L. Hartley, (Eds.), *Readings in Social Psychology*, New York: Holt, 1958, 359-370.

Winch, R.F. The relation between loss of a parent and progress in courtship. *Journal of Social Psychology*, 1949, *29*, 51-56.

Winch, R.F. Some data bearing on the Oedipus hypothesis. *Journal of Abnormal and Social Psychology*, 1950, *45*, 481-489.

Winch, R.F. Further data and observations on the Oedipus hypothesis: The consequences of an inadequate hypothesis. *American Sociological Review*, 1951, *16*, 784-795.

Winch, R.F. *Identification and its familial determinants.* New York: Bobbs-Merrill, 1962.

Witkin, H.A. The problem of individuality in development. In B. Kaplan & S. Wapner, (Eds.), *Perspectives in psychological theory*, New York: International Universities Press, 1960, 335-361.

Wohlford, P., Santrock, J.W., Berger, S.E., & Liberman, D. Older brothers' influence on sex-typed, aggressive, and dependent behavior in father-absent children. *Developmental Psychology*, 1971, *4*, 124-134.

Wright, B. & Tuska, S. The nature and origin of feeling feminine. *British Journal of Social Psychology*, 1966, *5*, 140-149.

Wylie, H.L. & Delgado, R.A. A pattern of mother-son relationship involving the absence of the father. *American Journal of Orthopsychiatry*, 1959, *29*, 644-649.

Wynn, M. *Fatherless families.* London: Michael Joseph, 1964.

Yarrow, L.J. Separation from parents during early childhood. In M.L. Hoffman & L.W. Hoffman (Eds.), *Review of child develop-*

ment research, Vol. 1. New York: Russell Sage Foundation, 1964, 89-136.

Zeichner, A. Psychosexual identification in paranoid schizophrenia. *Journal of Projective Techniques,* 1955, *19,* 67-77.

Zeichner, A. Conception of masculine and feminine roles in paranoid schizophrenics. *Journal of Projective Techniques,* 1956, *20,* 348-354.

Zelditch, M., Jr. Role differentiation in the nuclear family: a comparative study. In T. Parsons and R.F. Bales (Eds.), *Family, socialization and interaction process.* New York: Free Press, 1955.

Indexes

Author Index

183

Subject Index

Orphanages, 16, 61. *See also* Institutionalized children

Overcompensatory masculinity. *See* Compensatory masculinity

Overdependence, 87. *See also* Dependence, Maternal overprotection

Parental interaction, 24, 26-27, 35, 40, 41, 44, 55, 78-79, 80-81, 83-86, 95, 106, 112-113, 115-117, 118, 124-125, 128, 129-130

Parents Without Partners, 134. *See also* Husbandless mothers

Parsonian theory, 23, 104, 106-107

Paternal. *See also* Father

Paternal differentiation, 97, 107-108, 125

Paternal rejection, 27, 45, 49, 68, 115

Patriarchal, 35, 36

Peace Corps, 76

Peers, 9, 17-18, 47, 68-70, 80, 90-92, 101

Physique, 41-42, 48, 52, 86, 90, 105

Polygamous families, 65, 67. *See also* Cross-cultural research

Popularity. *See* Interpersonal relations, Peer group

Population explosion, 128

Postpartum taboos, 7, 91. *See also* Cross-cultural research

Power theory. *See* Social power theory

Practical applications, 127-134

Preference. *See* Sex-role preference

Prenatal factors, 122, 123

Preschool years. *See* Developmental stages; Early father-absence

Projective tests, 19. *See also* Blacky Test, Franck Test; Human-figure drawings; TAT

Psychoanalytic theory. *See* Freudian Theory

Psychopathology, 76-81, 96, 113-117, 121, 129

Psychosis, 77-78, 116, 117, 125. *See also* Psychopathology

Psychosomatic problems, 88

Psychotherapy, 129-131, 133

Puerto Rican children, 14

Punishment. *See* Limit-setting

Q-sort, 99

Rating Scales, 11-12

Reading, 56, 116. *See also* Cognitive functioning

Reasons for father-absence, 15, 84, 121. *See also* Divorce; Death of father; Types of father-absence

Reinforcement. *See* Imitation; Maternal encouragement

Rejection. *See* Maternal rejection; Paternal rejection

Religious factors, 84. *See also* Sociocultural factors

Responsibility, 73-74, 80

Retardation. *See* Mental retardation

Rogers Test of Personality Adjustment, 96

Role playing, 130

Role theory, 23, 24, 32, 33

Rorschach. *See* Projective tests

Rosenberg and Sutton-Smith Play and Game List, 11

Schizophrenia, 78-79, 116-117. *See also* Psychopathology

School-related behavior, 17, 55-63, 73, 76, 77, 80, 83, 89, 117, 122, 131-132. *See also* Cognitive functioning

Self concept, 18, 67, 73, 110, 114, 115, *See also* Sex role orientation

Self control, 37, 64-66, 103, 113

Sensitivity, 104, 113, 128. *See also* Interpersonal relations

Sex anxiety, 28. *See also* Anxiety; Sex-role conflicts

Sex differences, 11, 39-41, 44, 59, 85, 87, 90, 99, 108, 114, 116, 120, 126-127

Sex-role adoption, 9, 11, 12, 13, 18, 25, 26, 30, 31, 32, 39, 47-53, 98

Sex-role awareness, 8, 9, 45, 57-58

Sex-role conflicts, 7, 90-93, 96, 109. *See also* Anxiety; Compensatory masculinity

Sex-role development. *See* Sex-role adoption; Sex-role orientation; Sex-role patterns; Sex-role preference; Sexual behavior

Sex-role measurement, 10-12, 121

Sex-role orientation, 4, 5, 6, 8, 10, 13, 18, 25, 26, 30, 43-45, 48, 49-53, 58, 72, 95, 98, 103, 110, 114

Sex-role patterns, 49-53

Sex-role preference, 6, 8, 9, 11, 13, 18, 25, 26, 30, 39-40, 45-47, 48, 49-53, 58, 91, 98, 103, 108, 110

Sexual behavior, 21-22, 71-73, 80, 91-92, 96, 106, 110-111, 118

Siblings, 15, 16-17, 47, 104, 116, 120

Social class. *See* Socioeconomic status

Social learning theory, 43

Social power theory, 23-24, 32, 33. *See also* Father's power

Sociocultural background, 4, 7, 9, 13-15, 25, 38-39, 41, 53, 57, 58, 62-67, 84-85, 88-91, 101, 103-104, 112, 117, 120, 125-126

Socioeconomic status, 13-15, 18, 35-37, 57, 58, 62-63, 66-67, 78, 84-85, 89-91, 104-105, 125-126. *See also* Sociocultural background
Somatotypes. *See* Physique
Sports. *See* Athletics
Status envy theory, 22, 23
Stepfathers, 66, 123-124
Strong Vocational Interest Blank, 11, 16, 29
Substitute parents. *See* Surrogate models
Superego. *See* Conscience development
Surrogate models, 14, 15-18, 49, 66, 85, 120, 122, 123-124, 130-132, 133, 134. *See also* Peer group; Siblings

TAT, 10, 29, 31
Teachers, 16, 63, 131-132. *See also* Education, School-related behavior
Temperment. *See* Constitutional factors
Terman and Miles Interest Inventory, 11
Therapy. *See* Psychotherapy
Time perception, 65
Toy preference. *See* Sex-role preference

Transsexual, 92
Trust, 6, 64, 65
Types of father-absence, 15, 120, 124, 133. *See also* Reasons for father-absence

Unemployment, 76

Verbal ability, 3, 59, 60, 62, 63, 116. *See also* Cognitive functioning

War, 2, 15
Warmth. *See* Maternal nurturance; Paternal nurturance
Welfare, 132
West Indian children. *See* Caribbean children
WISC, 57
Witkin's rod and frame test, 12, 60. *See also* Field dependence-independence
Women's liberation movement, 128
Working class. *See* Socioeconomic status
Working mothers. *See* Maternal employment

YMCA, 131

About the Author

Henry B. Biller is an Associate Professor in the Psychology Department, University of Rhode Island, Kingston, Rhode Island. He was a Phi Betta Kappa, Magna Cum Laude graduate from Brown University, 1962; a United States Public Health Service predoctoral fellow at Duke University, 1962-1965; a clinical psychology intern at the Emma Pendleton Bradley Hospital, 1965-1966; and a United States Public Health Service predoctoral research fellow at Duke, 1966-1967. After receiving his Ph.D. from Duke in 1967 he was a faculty member at the University of Massachusetts (1967-1969) and at George Peabody College (1969-1970). His academic positions have all included participation in University affiliated mental health facilities (University of Massachusetts Child Guidance Clinic; George Peabody College Child Study Center; University of Rhode Island Psychology Clinic). He is a consultant to the Emma Pendleton Bradley Hospital, Riverside, Rhode Island, and the Veterans Administration Hospital, Providence, Rhode Island. Dr. Biller is the author of more than thirty scientific articles, and is currently working on a second book, *Sex Role and Personality Development.*